THE ART OF Self-Insurance

THE ART OF SELF-INSURANCE

by David A. North and Catherine D. Bennett

For information contact: Director of Corporate Communications, Sedgwick Claims Management Services, Inc., 1100 Ridgeway Loop Road, Memphis, TN 38120. Telephone 901 415-7400.

Printed in the United States of America.

ISBN 0-9726207-0-2

Preface & Acknowledgements

Through the years, our experience has shown that self-insurance can be a valuable financial and risk management tool no matter what the state of the economy or condition of the insurance market. Organizations of many different types have continuously found this classic risk financing strategy to be an effective tool for achieving cost savings and enhancing program control.

During the extended soft insurance market of the 'nineties and somewhat beyond, however, the competitive pricing of traditional fixed cost insurance plans and other risk financing devices crowded self-insurance from the limelight. Consequently many of today's up and coming specialists have had little opportunity for personal involvement with a self-insured program. Now that the environment of risk financing has changed emphatically, we believe it is timely to revisit this proven technique. The result of this conviction is the book we have entitled *The Art of Self-Insurance.*

Our goal in *The Art of Self-Insurance* is to provide risk managers, insurance professionals and financial officers with a greater level of comfort in assessing the potential of self-insurance for their organizations. We want our readers to become familiar with what it takes to establish and maintain a self-insurance program over the long term. We have emphasized fundamental concepts and practical applications. The chapters unfold chronologically through the cycle of information gathering, evaluation and implementation. For purposes of clarity and consistency, we have structured our discussion around the example of workers' compensation, although the utility of self-insurance is by no means limited to that arena.

Self-insurance is not the right answer for every risk financing situation. No single solution is. But self-insurance is an approach to be strongly considered, particularly for large risks characterized by high frequency and low severity. The decision to self-insure should be based on a balanced consideration of the distinctive risk, financial, regulatory and cultural imperatives of each organization. While our examination of self-insurance necessarily addresses technical and financial considerations, we hope our readers will discover that there truly is an art to designing and managing a successful self-insurance program.

We have benefited greatly in the endeavor of authorship from the generous collaboration of many outstanding professionals. For their invaluable advice and assistance through the burdensome process of manuscript review we would like to acknowledge and thank John Blassick of Risk Solutions, Inc. and Kim Norris, Paul Posey and Robert Wisecarver of Sedgwick Claims Management Services, Inc. We are also grateful to Timothy Brady, Richard Colantuono and Timothy Crombie of Marsh, Inc. for their insightful consultations on the finer points of insurance and claims, and to Brenda Corey of Sedgwick CMS for sharing her knowledge of regulatory matters. Michael Bennett of Cost Control Concepts, Inc. supplied creative direction and clear, clean design for the book. Bill Ross of Bill Ross Illustration captured the odyssey of our risk manager in a series of wonderfully whimsical illustrations. Finally, we wish to thank three additional Sedgwick CMS colleagues for helping us reach the finish line: Amanda Griffin for her eagle-eyed proof reading, Jonathan Mast for his careful management of production and distribution, and Frank Huffman for laboring with us throughout as project manager and editor. These friends contributed greatly to the merits of this publication. We reserve accountability for its shortcomings to ourselves.

We hope you enjoy *The Art of Self-Insurance* and that it will be a resource to which you turn for many years to come.

Sincerely,

DAVID A. NORTH   CATHERINE D. BENNETT

The risk management community has a rich heritage of pioneers. Four such pioneers, particular friends of the authors, are noteworthy among those who have shaped our thinking about risk financing, loss prevention, claims and technology, the pillars of a strong self-insurance program.

Dedication

CHUCK MATHERS' career spanned thirty-two years during which time he led thinking on funding techniques for clients of Johnson & Higgins and later Marsh. Chuck understood the concepts of self-insurance, and as the self-insurance practice leader at J&H generously shared his wisdom with the new kids.

HARRY TABACK knew the best claim was one that never occurred. During nearly thirty years of service at Marsh he led the safety practice and mentored hundreds of safety professionals through whose efforts unnumbered workers lead healthier, more productive and comfortable lives.

SUE SAUER was not bound by traditional silo thinking. She learned her craft as a human resource manager and later a workers' compensation manager. She taught us how the concepts of quality process and benchmarking produce better results for both employers and claimants in the administration of workers' compensation claims.

GARY LASKO was either the most business-savvy technology leader we have known, or the most technology-savvy business leader. As director of information systems for Sedgwick North America and later as corporate technical director of global technology services with Marsh, he kept the dialogue between commerce and technology lively, constructive and mutually respectful.

Chuck, Harry, Sue and Gary perished in the attacks on the World Trade Center on September 11, 2001, along with scores of other highly valued friends and professional colleagues. This book is dedicated to them in acknowledgement of their lasting contributions to our education and in appreciation of their unforgettable friendships.

About the Authors

David A. North

David A. North is president and CEO of Sedgwick Claims Management Services, Inc.

Mr. North has over twenty years of experience in risk management services. He joined Sedgwick CMS in 1995 to provide overall corporate leadership in strategic development and growth.

Prior to joining Sedgwick CMS, Mr. North was the global practice leader for risk services at a major brokerage and risk management consulting firm. There, he led the development of a total cost of risk strategy that included the property and casualty loss control services, claims management and consulting, risk management information services, structured settlements, law advisory and workers' compensation consulting. These services were expanded around the world under his leadership.

Mr. North has consistently pioneered service methodologies rooted in the concept of quality. His work has been based on benchmarking, best practices, process analysis and team-based problem solving. He has consulted with many Fortune 500 companies on innovative techniques to control costs including twenty-four hour care and services.

Mr. North is a frequent speaker at CPCU chapters and at national and local RIMS meetings. He developed and taught the American Management Association course on Advanced Risk Management Strategies: Managing the Total Cost of Risk. He serves as Chairman of the Board of the Integrated Benefits Institute.

Catherine D. Bennett

Catherine D. Bennett is vice president and communications director of Cost Control Concepts, Inc. In this role, she combines industry expertise with award-winning design and advertising to develop and produce creative marketing and communications materials.

Prior to establishing the company, Ms. Bennett served as a vice president at a major brokerage and risk management consulting firm. In this position, she was responsible for providing consulting, sales, and service assistance to large accounts. During her tenure in the insurance industry, she has served as a broker, account manager, and a risk management consultant specializing in self-insurance, alternative risk financing programs, and cost management practices.

Ms. Bennett is a frequent speaker at seminars and conferences, and she has published numerous articles appearing in *Business Insurance, National Underwriter,* and the *Global Risk Manager.* She holds both the Certified Property and Casualty Underwriter (CPCU) and Associate in Risk Management (ARM) professional designations.

Ms. Bennett is a graduate of Vanderbilt University with a B.A. in economics and related work in communications. She earned an M.B.A. from Vanderbilt's Owen Graduate School of Management where her concentrations were marketing and human resource management.

TABLE OF CONTENTS

Hᴀᴠᴇ ʏᴏᴜ ᴇᴠᴇʀ ᴡᴏɴᴅᴇʀᴇᴅ ᴀʙᴏᴜᴛ ꜱᴇʟꜰ-ɪɴꜱᴜʀᴀɴᴄᴇ? Tʜᴇꜱᴇ ᴘᴇᴏᴘʟᴇ ʜᴀᴠᴇ.

The Chief Financial Officer: Managing Cash More Effectively

The idea was quite intriguing to the young CFO. Keisha Greene had assumed the executive position three years earlier and had been notably recognized for her uncanny approach to corporate finance. Dining with a friend in the insurance industry, she contemplated the idea of self-insurance.

CHAPTER ONE:

Considering Self-Insurance

Imagine investing loss reserves until actual claim payments become due and then utilizing the resulting investment income to offset other program expenses. Clearly, this type of arrangement would benefit her corporation's present financial position. She became eager to learn more.

The risk manager was under the impression that the purchase of insurance was a fairly straightforward transaction. But, how do you explain a 150% premium increase to your boss?

The Insurance Broker: Beating the Market Cycles

The conference room was silent as the risk manager read the insurance quote summary from his broker, Scott Malone. The risk manager was under the impression that the purchase of insurance was a fairly straightforward transaction. But, how do you explain a 150% premium increase to your boss? Yes, there had been several losses in the Pittsburgh facility, but the remaining locations had shown considerable improvement in their loss reduction efforts. When the risk manager placed the quote aside, Scott leaned over the conference table and said, "So, let me tell you about self-insurance."

The Risk Manager: Achieving Employee Relations Goals Through Claims Handling

The morning headlines read, "Community Rallies Around Injured Worker." The single mother had suffered a severe hand injury while working on the assembly line. Monthly bills were quickly coming due. She had not heard from the insurance company. Filled with fear and apprehension, the injured woman called a local attorney for assistance, and the story hit the media. Now the newly promoted risk manager, Michael Sanchez, was struggling with the explosive consequences of a badly-handled claims situation. Faced with negative media coverage and a litigated claim, Michael knew this could not happen again. He began to search for ways to gain greater control over his company's claims activities. When an industry colleague suggested self-insurance as a possible solution that would put him in the driver's seat in addressing future claims situations, he immediately decided to find out more.

These stories reflect the growing interest in self-insurance among financial and risk management professionals. Self-insurance is often thought of as a complicated and somewhat obscure risk financing program, but in reality, it is simply a well-devised plan in which an organization chooses to pay for its own losses. The potential payoff and rewards associated with this type of program can be significant.

Today's market conditions have stimulated an increased interest in self-insurance. Many organizations are

Self-insurance is often thought of as a complicated and somewhat obscure risk financing program, but in reality, it is simply a well-devised plan in which an organization chooses to pay for its own losses.

presently faced with rising insurance prices and shrinking insurance capacity. The property and casualty industry has been hammered by economic uncertainty, fluctuating investment income, unsympathetic legislative attitudes, broadening definitions of coverage, and unimaginable catastrophes. These are the conditions under which self-insurance thrives.

Self-insurance is a classic risk management tool to be considered whatever the state of the economy or whether the insurance market is in an up or down cycle.

Self-insurance is a classic risk management tool to be considered whatever the state of the economy or whether the insurance market is in an up or down cycle. As the opening stories portray, Keisha, Scott and Michael will learn that self-insurance can be a powerful solution to a host of risk management challenges. Self-insurance offers a potential means for lowering overall program costs, achieving a greater degree of independence from the commercial marketplace, and achieving more effective management of claims activities. Most self-insured companies share a common goal in simply wanting to exert a greater degree of control over their risk management programs.

As a result, chief financial officers, risk managers, insurance brokers and other industry professionals need a working knowledge and fundamental understanding of self-insurance programs and principles.

The purpose of this book is to provide today's financial and risk management professionals with an overview of important self-insurance strategies and concepts. This information will enable them to consider the self-insurance alternative more easily and ultimately to determine whether self-insurance might benefit their organizations.

This book will help its readers address four key questions:

1. What is self-insurance?
2. Is self-insurance a good option for my organization?
3. How do I set up an effective self-insurance program?
4. How do I manage a self-insurance program for ongoing success?

The first portion of the book examines such issues as various types of self-insurance arrangements, key advantages and disadvantages associated with a self-insurance plan, state rules and regulations governing self-insurers, and important issues to consider when evaluating the feasibility of a self-insurance program.

The second portion of the book deals with how to manage a successful self-insurance program. It explores such issues as analyzing risk management data and information, building a strong safety culture, streamlining the claims management process, and launching a successful communications campaign.

There truly is an art to establishing and maintaining a self-insurance plan. It is an art that incorporates an analysis of both quantitative and

There truly is an art to establishing and maintaining a self-insurance plan. It is an art which incorporates an analysis of both quantitative and qualitative issues.

qualitative issues. For those who master this craft and learn how to draw upon self-insurance as an effective risk financing strategy, the potential payoff can be significant.

Take time to explore self-insurance and see how this alternative program can be used to enhance almost any risk management landscape.

CHAPTER TWO:

Defining Self-Insurance

CHAPTER OVERVIEW: *The term self-insurance has been used loosely through the years to describe a wide range of risk financing plans involving self-funding of selected classes of losses. Whatever the arrangement, most self-insured organizations share a common goal in wanting to obtain greater control over their risk management programs through risk retention. One of the more common self-insurance plans, qualified self-insurance, is a well-defined program in which a company chooses to pay its own losses up to a specified amount. Most self-insureds purchase excess insurance to limit their exposure to unacceptable levels of losses. An organization must submit an application and comply with established state rules and regulations to achieve and maintain self-insured status. A well-managed self-insurance program offers the potential for significant cost savings as compared to some of the more traditional insurance plans.*

THROUGH THE YEARS, THE TERM "SELF-INSURANCE" HAS BEEN USED LOOSELY TO DESCRIBE A WIDE VARIETY OF RISK FINANCING ARRANGEMENTS THROUGH WHICH ORGANIZATIONS PAY ALL OR A SIGNIFICANT PORTION OF THE COSTS OF SELECTED CLASSES OF THEIR OWN LOSSES. These range from a small business assuming a low dollar deductible on its auto physical damage losses to a multi-national corporation insuring its liability exposure through an offshore captive insurance company. Similarly, companies utilizing retrospectively-rated plans, large deductible plans or qualified self-insurance plans often use the generic term self-insurance to describe their risk funding programs. The term has also been applied to some types of association programs in which a number of companies pool their respective risks and agree to pay for member losses. In extreme circumstances, self-insurance has been interchanged with the term "going bare," coined to describe those situations where no loss funding arrangement has been provided at all.

A Common Self-Insurance Goal: Greater Control. Whatever the arrangement, companies that have turned to self-insurance programs in recent decades have typically shared a common goal – greater control. A successful self-insurance plan can give organizations greater control over expected losses and related program expenses; insurance market cycles resulting in fluctuations in pricing and coverage availability; and the overall delivery of risk management services.

Whatever the arrangement, companies that have turned to self-insurance programs in recent decades have typically shared a common goal – greater control.

Unregulated Lines. Self-insurers have a high degree of flexibility in program design and structure. Many lines of coverage such as general liability, professional liability, products liability, property and crime are considered to be unregulated lines of coverage. They are not subject to state regulations when self-insured. There are no governmental restrictions on investments, financial audits, claims reporting, or security for paying claims.

Regulated Lines. Where legal responsibility is created by statute, as in the case of workers' compensation and automobile liability, self-insurers are subject to very specific state regulations. These are referred to as regulated lines of coverage. Self-insurers of these lines of coverage face state reporting requirements and must demonstrate they have the financial wherewithal to pay losses. Requirements and regulations vary considerably from state to state.

Characteristics Conducive to Self-Insurance

Certain lines of coverage lend themselves to self-insurance more readily than others. For example, lines of coverage characterized by high frequency and low severity of claims are good candidates for self-insurance. This is because the volume of claims tends to be relatively predictable and excess insurance can be purchased to address any potentially severe or catastrophic cases.

Characteristics of Good Self-Insurance Candidates

- High claims frequency
- Low claims severity
- Extended payout schedule

Also, lines of coverage characterized by an extended payout schedule are good candidates for self-insurance. This is because the self-insurer retains control of the loss reserves until claims are actually paid and has the opportunity to invest those funds for the benefit of the organization. Under a traditional insurance plan, the insured pays the premium up front and the insurance company benefits from use of these funds until claims are paid.

Workers' compensation exhibits both of these characteristics. First, it is a relatively stable line of coverage in terms of predictability of losses and the nature of losses. Second, industry data indicate that typically only 25% of estimated ultimate losses are paid out within the first twelve months of the policy year. Such payout estimates apply to aggregate data as opposed to individual claims. Also, workers' compensation benefits are determined and limited by state statutes. Litigation is less likely to impact workers' compensation than some liability lines of coverage. As a result, workers' compensation costs are generally more predictable, and this added stability makes workers' compensation especially desirable to self-insure.

While general liability and professional liability claims are characterized by extended payout schedules, the frequency and severity of these types of losses are less predictable. In addition, these claims are often litigated, injecting increased levels of cost variability into the equation. Still, many companies have elected to self-insure these lines of coverage due to the high cost and in some cases, unavailability of commercial insurance during hard market cycles.

In its truest sense, qualified self-insurance is a well-defined financing mechanism in which the self-insured organization pays for its own losses.

Having examined a generalized definition of self-insurance, it is important to consider a more precise definition of the term qualified self-insurance. Using workers' compensation as an example, this book will address key characteristics associated with qualified self-insurance plans; examples of state rules and regulations with which self-insured organizations must comply; how qualified self-insurance compares to alternative risk financing plans; and how to ensure and maintain success once a qualified self-insurance plan is put in place.

Key Characteristics of Qualified Self-Insurance Plans

Key Characteristics of Qualified Self-Insurance Plans

- Self-insured must comply with state rules and regulations
- Self-insured pays for own losses
- Risk retention level is predetermined
- Excess insurance is purchased to limit exposure
- Cost management program can be customized
- Controlling losses results in immediate savings
- Self-insured retains control of loss reserves
- Direct correlation exists between losses and program costs
- Management must be active and involved

In its truest sense, qualified self-insurance is a well-defined financing mechanism in which the self-insured organization pays for its own losses in regulated lines of coverage. In most cases, a self-insurer will specify the amount of losses it wishes to retain and purchase excess insurance for all losses exceeding that level.

As the name implies, a qualified self-insurer must qualify or comply with the rules and regulations in each state in which it plans to self-insure its workers' compensation losses. This typically includes completing a state application for self-insurance, meeting the state's financial, security and excess insurance requirements to ensure payment of claims, and filing requested information and forms such as financial statements, claims reports, or service plans. Notably, these requirements and regulations vary considerably from state to state.

Qualified self-insurance offers a self-insured the opportunity to generate substantial program savings as a result of a more streamlined administrative program and favorable loss experience.

One of the key characteristics of a qualified self-insurance plan is that the self-insurer is able to put together a completely customized cost management program. Service firms with specialized industry expertise can be identified and only those services valued by the self-insurer need to be purchased. The ability to tap industry specific expertise and high quality professionals can be extremely valuable in such fields as loss control and claims management. To the extent a self-insurer can control losses, the company can capitalize upon immediate cost savings opportunities.

Additionally, a self-insurer retains control of the loss reserve dollars until payments are actually made. The self-insurer can invest these funds until claims payments are made and benefit from resulting investment income.

One of the most attractive features of qualified self-insurance is the potential for cost savings. Immediate savings are achieved if a self-insurer can prevent accidents and manage accident costs when they do occur. A well-designed excess insurance program can further protect a self-insured should losses escalate or a catastrophic event occur.

Qualified self-insurance offers a self-insured the opportunity to generate substantial program savings as a result of a more streamlined administrative program and favorable loss experience. It requires a much higher degree of active involvement on the part of the self-insured, and this generally results in fewer accidents and lower losses.

Rules and regulations differ from state to state, both in terms of qualifying and maintaining the program; however, the potential benefits associated with a successful plan can certainly outweigh the added risk and responsibility. The longevity of self-insurance and its prevalence during both hard and soft market conditions speaks of its effectiveness as a strategic risk management tool.

C HAPTER OVERVIEW: *A well-designed and well-managed qualified self-insurance program can result in many benefits to the self-insured organization. Key advantages associated with such a program include potential cost savings, insulation from market cycles, and improved cash flow. A badly designed, poorly run program can have negative financial consequences for an organization. Some common disadvantages include increased administrative requirements and possible exposure to unanticipated loss costs. The key is recognizing the potential pitfalls associated with such a plan and taking appropriate actions to minimize any potential negative effects.*

CHAPTER THREE

Weighing the Pros and Cons of Self-Insurance

A WELL-STRUCTURED QUALIFIED SELF-INSURANCE PLAN CAN SERVE AS A VERY EFFECTIVE AND EFFICIENT MEANS OF RISK FINANCING. Before embarking upon such a plan, of course, organizations should examine how such a plan operates and how it relates to their philosophy and goals. To gain a better understanding of qualified self-insurance, an overview of key advantages and disadvantages of this type of program is provided.

Self-Insurance Advantages

Potential cost savings. Many companies cite potential cost savings as their number one reason for self-insuring workers' compensation losses. Potential cost savings can result from reducing and controlling losses, increased awareness of safety and claims procedures, reduction in expenses associated with commercially insured plans, and the opportunity to generate investment income as a result of maintaining control of the loss reserves.

Market insulation. Another commonly stated reason for self-insurance is insulation from market cycles. These cycles result in fluctuations in pricing and coverage availability. For example, it is not uncommon for companies with poor loss experience to see renewal rates jump 50% to 100%. In extreme circumstances, the increase could be three or four times the original quote, if coverage is available at all. Self-insurance interjects some stability in what could otherwise be a wild market ride.

Self-Insurance Advantages:
- Potential cost savings
- Market insulation
- Improved cashflow
- Overhead expense reduction
- Customized services
- Increased awareness
- Immediate savings
- Improved public relations
- Improved Employee Satisfaction
- Coordination of benefits

Improved cash flow. Self-insurance is often applauded for its ability to improve a company's cash flow position. No pre-funding of losses is required as in the case of many traditional insurance plans, and no significant capital outlay is needed as in the case of establishing a captive insurance company.

The cash flow advantages of self-insurance become especially noticeable in those lines of coverage with extended payout schedules. In some cases, loss payments are spread over eight to ten years.

While funds must remain relatively liquid for loss payment, to the extent the investment dollars are carefully managed, the resulting investment income can be used to offset other program expenses.

Under an insured plan, it is the insurance company that retains control of the loss reserves and benefits from any resulting investment income. Generally, the premium is due on day one or payments are simply spread over the course of the policy year.

Overhead Expense Reduction. Although administrative responsibilities increase, self-insureds typically enjoy lower operating costs in comparison to the corresponding expenses associated with a traditional insurance program. Many of the same services are required but often a self-insurer can streamline the service process as opposed to supporting a large corporate staff of underwriters, accountants, claims adjusters, safety engineers, attorneys, and administrative assistants. Under a qualified self-insurance plan a self-insurer may, depending upon state law, also eliminate or reduce expenses such as premium taxes, rating bureau fees, residual market loadings, second injury funds, solvency funds, and insurance company profit and acquisition costs.

Self-insurers can target resources at the areas likely to generate the greatest return on investment and have the biggest impact on cost savings. This type of customization and control presents yet another opportunity for a self-insurer to achieve operating efficiencies.

Customized Services. Under a self-insured program, a self-insured can implement a completely customized service package. While essentially the same services provided under a commercially insured plan must be applied to a self-insurance plan, self-insurers have the flexibility to select firms that have specialized expertise and experience specific to their industries. They can target resources at the areas likely to generate the greatest return on investment and have the biggest impact on cost savings. This type of customization and control presents yet another opportunity for a self-insurer to achieve operating efficiencies.

Contrastingly, most insurance companies must provide loss control and claims handling services suitable for a wide range of industries. The safety needs of a hospital are very different than those of a fast food restaurant. Insurance companies may not provide the customized, detailed loss reports necessary to enable an organization to prevent and manage future occurrences. Also, there is less opportunity to carefully select an account team under an insured plan that really embodies the self-insured's service philosophy. The same concept applies to the procurement of actuarial, accounting, legal, and risk management information services.

Increased awareness. Once a firm implements a self-insurance program, there tends to be a shift in thinking. The organization is clearly spending its own money rather than the insurance company's. There is a heightened sense of awareness of the company's cost management programs. Adherence to safe work practices becomes a greater priority. Prompt reporting of claims receives more immediate attention. Management closely monitors loss costs and any resulting impact on earnings. Because of this program ownership, a renewed emphasis is placed on cost control techniques that can result in long-term savings and improvements in the corporate safety culture.

Once a firm implements a self-insurance program, there tends to be a shift in thinking. The organization is clearly spending its own money rather than the insurance company's.

Immediate savings. A self-insured who successfully controls losses and aggressively manages operating expenses enjoys immediate program savings. Fewer dollars are paid out during the current policy year. Under a commercially insured plan, it often takes many months and sometimes years before successful program results are reflected in favorable premium pricing. Even the calculation of an insured's experience modification factor is based on a three year rolling average of losses. A single year in which loss costs drop significantly will have only a modest effect on the experience modification factor and resulting premium calculation.

Improved Public Relations. A self-insurance program offers an organization greater control over the manner in which claims are handled. Occasionally, an accident may occur which demands extreme sensitivity in resolving the claims situation. The circumstances might involve a prominent customer or have serious ramifications for an organization's public image. A self-insured has greater control over how claims are handled, while an insurance company claims administrator may be rewarded for simply resolving a claim quickly, with little regard for the possibility of unintended, adverse consequences.

Increased Employee Satisfaction. Increased employee satisfaction is another positive benefit arising from a well-administered self-insurance program. When claims are perceived to be handled fairly and efficiently, employees show a greater sense of overall satisfaction with the process. This can be a very important advantage in today's environment where recruitment and retention of quality employees is almost a universal goal.

Coordination of Benefits. Because self-insureds have greater control over their claims handling programs, they have a better opportunity to coordinate workers' compensation with other benefits programs. Integrated disability management programs which include a comprehensive integration of workers' compensation, liability and disability are gaining popularity. Many employers are finding it to be more efficient for them and less stressful for injured workers if all such claims are managed on an integrated basis. Because self-insureds have more control over the administration of their claims, they may have more latitude to explore advanced techniques such as integrated disability management.

Self-Insurance Disadvantages

While qualified self-insurance is characterized by many positive attributes, it is not a silver bullet program to be implemented in all circumstances. It is equally important that a company understand common pitfalls associated with self-insurance so that an informed decision can be made. Key considerations and drawbacks surrounding a self-insurance program must be identified and understood. A summary of common disadvantages of self-insurance follows.

Increased Administrative Responsibilities. While qualified self-insurance provides companies greater control over their programs, the price associated with this attribute is increased administrative responsibilities. Self-insureds may either administer a program internally or contract with external service providers. Many self-insureds employ a combination of internal staff and external service firms, thereby playing to their firms' strengths and resource capabilities.

While qualified self-insurance provides companies greater control over their programs, the price associated with this attribute is increased administrative responsibilities.

Whether self-administered or employing a third party administrator, self-insureds are responsible for meeting all state requirements including maintenance and submission of requested loss data and financial information, completion of state filings and forms, and timely payment of state taxes and assessments. The increased administrative responsibilities in dealing with the

Self-Insurance Disadvantages:

- Increased administration
- Possible spikes in losses
- Pricing of other coverages
- Long-term commitment
- Sensitive employee relations
- Release of financial statements
- Certificates of self-insurance
- Security costs
- Excess coverage
- Tax implications

state authorities, particularly assuming a multi-state self-insurance program, can be substantial.

In addition, a self-insured is responsible for identifying and selecting qualified vendors in the areas of program administration and cost management. Under an insurance program, most of these services are provided on a bundled basis by the insurance company. This includes claims, safety and loss control, actuarial and accounting, risk information, and legal services. Once service firms are selected, ongoing management of their performance is required to ensure the program's long-term success.

Also, a self-insured is still subject to some insurance marketing activities in the case of securing excess insurance and surety bonds. Underwriting submissions must be prepared and presented to the marketplace. Left unmanaged, the increase in administration could overshadow any potential program savings.

Possible Spikes in Losses. Self-insureds are subject to the effects of unanticipated losses and accidents. Losses may vary significantly from year to year, particularly in some of the relatively smaller programs. This may be due to a catastrophic occurrence or an aggregation of losses over the course of the policy year.

Losses may vary significantly from year to year, particularly in some of the relatively smaller programs.

A well-structured excess insurance program can provide some insulation from such swings; however, excess insurance is subject to market cycles which may impact pricing and availability of coverage. Also, surety bonds can be difficult to obtain during hard market conditions. Similarly, state taxes, assessments and fees are subject to constant change, thereby introducing additional variability into the cost equation.

In addition, the self-insured may suffer the adverse impact of a variation in payment of losses. For example, a line of coverage typically exemplifying a long tail payment pattern may be affected by extenuating circumstances which dictate more rapid claims payments.

By nature, self-insurance is a program for which budgeting is difficult, but there are methods for addressing this problem. In situations where cost predictability and budgeting is crucial, alternative funding programs can be considered. The design of an excess insurance program can also lower the cost variability associated with a self-insured plan.

Pricing of Other Coverages. Many organizations market their programs on a package basis. Underwriters are given the opportunity to bid on casualty lines including workers' compensation, general liability, and auto liability. By withdrawing workers' compensation, the underwriter loses profit potential and is forced to bid only on those lines of coverage exhibiting more variability and higher loss potential. As a result, program pricing associated with the remaining coverages may be higher than it would have been if workers' compensation had been included in the package. This potential cost inflation in the other lines of coverage must be

A company which decides to implement a qualified self-insurance program should do so with a long-term commitment to the funding mechanism. An organization should not expect to move back and forth between a self-insurance program and a commercially insured plan simply based on more competitive pricing and the state of the market.

recognized and factored into consideration when an organization elects to implement self-insurance. Such hidden increases may show up in increased tax multipliers, loss conversion factors, or basic premium factor charges.

It should also be recognized that some carriers will not unbundle the programs and services they offer. For those companies considering self-insurance, emphasis should be placed on identifying and selecting carriers and service providers that will help in the transition of the program and collaborate on putting together a plan that meets the company's strategic needs.

Long-term commitment. A company that decides to implement a qualified self-insurance program should do so with a long-term commitment to the funding mechanism. An organization should not expect to move back and forth between a self-insurance program and a commercially insured plan simply based on more competitive pricing and the state of the market.

The termination of a qualified self-insurance program brings with it costly consequences. The abandonment of the program procedures and systems can be expensive, and the return on investment to develop the systems is diminished or lost entirely. In addition, many states require that security remain in place until all claim payments are made. Sometimes this extends for many years.

Sensitive Employee Relations. Under a commercially insured plan, the insurance carrier can serve as a buffer between management and employees in potential claim disputes. It is the insurance carrier that bears the brunt of the blast when a claim is denied or perceived to be underpaid. An insurance company is not available as an intermediary under a self-insured program. The involvement of an independent third party administrator can mitigate the potential for friction between the employer and employee.

Release of Financial Statements. Qualified self-insurance is sometimes dismissed as a viable funding program by privately held firms because of the need to release certain financial information to the states. These financial records may become open documents and available to the public. Some privately held firms simply do not wish to share this sensitive information or make it available to competing firms for strategic purposes.

Today, there are increasing pressures on companies to fully disclose loss reserves and other payables to auditors and related parties. Accurate accounting practices must be employed.

Certificates of Self-Insurance. States typically issue qualified self-insurers certificates of self-insurance. However, these certificates may not be perceived and as readily accepted as traditional certificates of insurance issued by large, well-known insurance carriers. Some contractual arrangements require a prospective bidder to furnish certificates of insurance as a condition of employment.

Security. The cost of meeting state security requirements can be an important consideration for qualified self-insurers. Some states require security as a guarantee that self-insureds can meet the obligations of future claims payments. The amount and type of security varies by state and is dependent upon a number of factors including an organization's financial strength, expected losses and industry characteristics. Surety bonds, letters of credit, cash, or a combination of these instruments are typically used to fulfill a state's security requirements.

Over a period of years, these security requirements can place a significant burden on a self-insured's available credit line as letters of credit begin to exhibit a pyramiding effect.

Excess Coverage. Even though a self-insured is insulated from most insurance market conditions, many organizations purchase some type of excess insurance. Excess insurance is impacted by market cycles, and pricing and coverage availability can vary significantly. Specific excess insurance is purchased to limit the effects of a single loss, while aggregate excess is designed to cap the financial consequences of a series of losses over the course of the policy year. In a tight market, aggregate excess coverage may not be available, forcing the self-insured to accept a greater degree of risk than originally intended.

Tax Implications. Under a self-insured plan, a self-insurer may only take a tax deduction for paid losses and paid expenses. Loss reserves are not tax deductible until losses are paid. Any lines of coverage exhibiting extended payout profiles typically result in delayed deductions. Under a commercially insured plan, the entire premium is deductible in the year in which it is paid. It is not a matter of loss and expense deductibility but simply the timing of the deduction that varies among plans. As with any tax situation, it is necessary to consult certified public accountants and appropriate legal counsel before assuming any tax strategy.

STATE
LINE

CHAPTER **O**VERVIEW: *A company wanting to self-insure its workers' compensation losses must qualify in each state in which it wishes to pay its own claims. Self-insurance rules and regulations vary considerably among the states and are subject to change. Some of the key areas on which a potential self-insurer will want to focus are: the application process, periodic filings, taxes and assessments, security, excess insurance, minimum operational standards and business characteristics, average application approval time, and unique state requirements.*

C**HAPTER** F**OUR**:

Understanding State and Territorial Rules & Regulations

TO PROVIDE A BETTER UNDERSTANDING OF THE QUALIFICATION PROCESS, KEY AREAS HAVE BEEN IDENTIFIED AND ARE DISCUSSED BELOW. It is important to remember these areas differ by state and are subject to constant change by the states' governing bodies. Employers should consult their professional advisors and contact the states directly before undertaking any changes that would impact their specific programs.

A candidate for qualified self-insurance must file an application in each state in which it wishes to operate. These applications can be quite detailed and the accompanying information requested is often extensive.

Application Process. A candidate for qualified self-insurance must file an application in each state in which it wishes to operate. These applications can be quite detailed, and the accompanying information requested is often extensive.

Types of information typically requested by states include: certified financial statements, historical losses, payrolls, premiums, number of employees, locations of operations, directors and officers, and a description of the proposed cost management and service program. A filing fee sometimes accompanies the submission of a self-insurance application. For example, Colorado subjects self-insured applicants to a $2,000 filing fee. Louisiana charges $100 per application. Some states do not require an application fee.

Key Areas to Consider When Applying for Self-Insurance

- Application process
- Periodic filings
- Taxes and assessments
- Security requirements
- Excess insurance requirements
- Minimum requirements
- Average approval time
- Unique requirements

If approval is granted, a certificate of self-insurance is issued. The term of such certificates varies from state to state. Some states issue certificates of self-insurance that are continuous until cancelled or revoked while in other states, self-insurance certificates are subject to annual renewal.

Periodic Filings. Once self-insured status is achieved, self-insured companies must continue to meet state filing requirements. Again, there is little or no standardization among the states as to what information is needed. The State of Washington requires self-insurers to pay quarterly assessments based on claim costs and hours worked. Florida requires companies to submit a payroll report annually covering all of their self-insured operations in that state. Most third party administrators or brokers offer this service.

Taxes and Assessments. State taxes and assessments are levied against self-insurers to provide monies for second injury funds, administrative funds, or insolvency funds. They are typically calculated as a percentage of standard premium or based upon benefits paid by the self-insurer. In some states these amounts are nominal, while in others they can be significant. For example, South Carolina levies a 2.5% assessment on self-insurers based on the total cost of their self-insurance program. Delaware self-insurers must pay a 4% assessment based on manual premium rates and their payrolls.

Interestingly, large deductible plans initially escaped many of the taxes and assessments imposed on self-insured companies. Now, however, many states impose similar charges on large deductibles as well.

Security Requirements. A key objective of state regulatory authorities is to ensure that self-insurers can pay their own losses. Otherwise, the states must address the consequences of unpaid liabilities.

A key objective of state regulatory authorities is to ensure that a self-insurer can pay its own losses. Otherwise, the states must address the consequences of unpaid liabilities.

To ensure self-insured obligations are met, most states impose some type of security requirement on the self-insured. These requirements generally consist of surety bonds, letters of credit, governmental securities or cash.

The amount of security required varies by state and by applicant. When establishing security requirements, states typically look at such factors as the self-insured's financial position, historical losses, excess insurance program, industry, and experience classification. As a result, self-insureds must pay close attention to the market for surety bonds as well as to their own lines of credit.

In Michigan, the minimum security required is $100,000. This may be in the form of either a surety bond or letter of credit. In Tennessee, all self-insurers must post a surety bond of at least $500,000 from an A rated company licensed to write surety in Tennessee.

Excess Insurance Requirements. Most states require self-insureds to purchase some type of excess insurance. As with other regulatory requirements, the amounts and types of excess coverage differ by state.

Types of Excess Insurance

- **Specific Excess:** protects a self-insured against the financial consequences of a single high-dollar loss.

- **Aggregate Excess:** protects a self-insured against the financial consequences of an accumulation of many losses over the policy period.

Specific excess insurance protects a self-insured against the financial consequences of a single high dollar loss. It provides protection on a per occurrence basis. Aggregate excess protects the self-insured against the financial consequences of an accumulation of many losses over the stated retention level. Like the primary market, the pricing and availability of coverage in the excess market can vary significantly.

The need for excess insurance is evaluated on a case by case basis in Hawaii and may not be required in all circumstances. Contrastingly, Michigan generally requires that a self-insurer carry both specific excess and aggregate excess insurance. Most state authorities consider excess coverage in assessing a self-insured's overall financial ability to pay claims.

Minimum Requirements. To ensure the financial strength and longevity of a potential self-insured applicant, many states impose minimum business or operational standards on the proposed self-insured applicant. For example, the self-insured might have to meet minimum requirements with respect to financial condition and net worth, premium, number of employees, or number of years in business. In the State of Alabama, a self-insured applicant must have and maintain a net worth of not less than $5,000,000, a current assets to current liabilities ratio of at least 1.0, and a positive net income for the past three years.

Average Approval Time. States vary considerably in the average time needed to review self-insured applications. As a result, a potential self-insured should allow ample time if a program is being considered for the upcoming policy year.

To ensure the financial strength and longevity of a potential self-insured applicant, many states impose minimum business or operational standards on the proposed self-insured applicant.

Delaware has a remarkably quick turnaround time with an average approval taking about two weeks. New York advises that applications should be submitted approximately four months prior to the desired effective date of self-insurance.

Unique Requirements. It is important for a self-insured or their representative to contact each state directly and request a copy of the states' rules, regulations, and required forms. Some states have very unique requirements. As an example, the State of Tennessee requires self-insureds to file an anti-fraud plan.

The compilation of requested data and information for a multi-state operation can be very time consuming. Moreover, state requirements are subject to constant change. A self-insured must have the resources to sufficiently address the states' regulations, both at the onset of the program and in its ongoing maintenance.

CHAPTER OVERVIEW: *Because of the long-term commitment required and the loss sensitive nature of the plan, the decision to become a qualified self-insurer must be carefully*

CHAPTER FIVE:

Exploring the Feasibility of Qualified Self-Insurance

considered. A multi-phase decision process minimizes surprises and helps ensure future program success. Some of the key areas to examine when conducting a preliminary assessment include: the organization's appetite for retaining risk, concentration of exposures, self-insurance regulatory climate, commitment to preventing and managing losses, excess insurance and bond market conditions, administrative capabilities and resources, and financial strengths and corporate objectives.

THE ATTRACTIVENESS OF MANY SELF-INSURED BENEFITS AND THE POSSIBILITY OF ACHIEVING GREATER PROGRAM CONTROL HAVE GENERATED A HIGH LEVEL OF INTEREST IN SELF-INSURANCE THROUGH THE YEARS. As with any long-term financial strategy, however, organizations should systematically evaluate the suitability of self-insurance for their individual circumstances.

Although there are many ways to approach the self-insurance decision, one alternative is to complete a preliminary assessment. If initial indications are favorable, the next step is to conduct a more formalized self-insurance feasibility study complete with an actuarial assessment of losses. If the results of the study indicate self-insurance is a promising alternative, a company should develop a very detailed and comprehensive implementation plan. By approaching this decision in a multi-phase fashion and relying on expert assistance when needed, a company enhances its chances of making a well-informed decision. This type of due diligence will increase the probability of a successful implementation phase and the achievement of long-term program objectives.

Preparing a Preliminary Assessment

It is relatively easy to conduct a preliminary assessment of the suitability of self-insurance for any given company. This initial assessment can usually be conducted by the in-house risk management staff, sometimes with assistance from a professional risk management consultant or broker.

Some key areas to examine during this preliminary stage include:

- What is the organization's appetite for retaining risk?
- In which states are business exposures concentrated and does the organization meet minimum state requirements?
- What is the self-insurance climate in those states where the firm wants to self-insure?
- Are losses under control and less than expected for similar size firms in the same industry?
- Is excess insurance readily available and at a reasonable price?
- How would the existing risk management department handle the increased administrative responsibilities posed by a self-insurance program?
- Does the company have the financial strength needed to become a qualified self-insurer?
- If the company is privately held, is management willing to release financial statements to the governing state authorities?

- What is the state of the surety marketplace?

- Can the firm meet state security requirements?

- How does self-insurance compare to other types of risk financing programs given stated organizational and financial objectives?

- Is self-insurance compatible with the anticipated growth or contraction of the company's operations?

- Are there any potential occupational disease exposures?

- Is senior management receptive to new risk management ideas and strategies?

This initial assessment can preserve valuable corporate time and resources. A firm that is otherwise a good candidate for self-insurance may have senior management that is uncomfortable with retained risk. Similarly, management of a privately held firm may immediately reject the idea of releasing financial statements. Alternatively, the firm may have widespread geographic distribution of employees and operating centers throughout the country but no single concentration of exposures in any one state to warrant self-insurance consideration.

If after a very thorough and honest self-assessment, indications are positive, the organization is advised to undertake a more formalized self-insurance feasibility study.

CHAPTER OVERVIEW: *Before launching a qualified self-insurance program, many organizations conduct a formalized feasibility study. These studies are generally produced with the assistance of highly trained actuaries and risk management consultants. Most feasibility studies include both an actuarial assessment of losses and a comparison of alternative risk financing plans. The results can assist an organization in making well-informed decisions about what level of losses to anticipate and how to effectively fund those losses.*

CHAPTER SIX:

Conducting a Formal Self-Insurance Feasibility Study

MOST ORGANIZATIONS ENGAGE SPECIALIZED ACTUARIAL AND RISK MANAGEMENT CONSULTANTS TO CONDUCT FORMALIZED SELF-INSURANCE FEASIBILITY STUDIES. These highly sophisticated studies are designed to address the viability of self-insurance for a specific organization and related risk financing issues.

The Value of a Formalized Feasibility Study. Most self-insurance feasibility studies cost thousands or tens of thousands of dollars depending upon the scope of the study, credentials and experience of professionals engaged, and number of states to be explored. There are a number of qualified professionals who perform these types of consulting studies on a regular basis and analyze the issues in a way that an informed decision can be made. This is an investment worth making given the long-term commitment required of a self-insurance plan and the potential benefits to be achieved by a well-conceived program.

Study Components. Most self-insurance feasibility studies contain:

- a loss forecast and related actuarial analyses,
- an identification and comparison of alternative risk financing programs suitable to the risk, and
- an assessment and summary of state self-insurance requirements in selected states.

Time Frame. Four to eight weeks is the typical timeframe required to complete most self-insurance feasibility studies. This lead time as well as the time needed for application approval in the various states must be factored in if a firm is considering self-insuring its losses for the upcoming policy year.

Information Requirements. The data required to complete such a study generally include: a loss development triangle showing unique patterns of loss development; a minimum of five years of historical losses as of their most recent evaluation date and a breakout of these losses by state; corresponding historical payrolls, employee counts, and premiums by state; a breakout of medical, indemnity and expense payments associated with the historical losses; a listing of large losses over the past five years with some description detail; copies of current workers' compensation policies; current program pricing; most recent certified financial statements; and corporate tax rate. Information pertaining to the risk management department's staffing, structure and capabilities is also useful in assessing how best to handle the additional administrative responsibilities of a self-insurance program.

In comparing the cost of a proposed self-insurance plan to alternative risk financing plans, estimated costs and plan factors can be obtained in several ways. First, actual market quotations may be used. Alternatively, educated estimates of plan factors and pricing may be used. While actual quotes provide a more realistic picture of the costs, a relative comparison of program costs based on program estimates reduces involvement with the insurance marketplace. Clearly, information gathering, compilation and analysis are central to the evaluation process.

> *Clearly, information gathering, compilation and analysis are central to the evaluation process.*

Loss Forecast. Once the data is collected, one of the first steps is for an actuary to make a projection of losses for the upcoming year. While the methodologies and actuarial techniques used are highly sophisticated, the actual loss forecasting concepts are relatively easy to grasp. First, historical losses are reviewed and analyzed. Losses for each of the prior policy years are developed to their estimated ultimate value using loss development factors. These loss development factors are designed to account for the adverse development of losses as well as for losses which have been incurred but not reported. The more recent the policy year, the greater the development that can be expected. Older years show less development as more claims are settled and the majority of losses are known and reported. Also, assuming early year loss reserves are established correctly, reserve levels for later years show less variability and change.

Once estimated ultimate losses are determined for each of the policy years, trend factors are applied to the estimates. Trend factors take into account medical inflation as well as changes in state benefit levels. Similarly, trend factors are applied to historical payroll figures.

Next, trended losses are compared to trended payrolls for each of the historical policy years to determine a loss rate per unit of exposure. These loss rates are carefully reviewed and analyzed, and a loss rate for the upcoming policy year is selected. It is reasonable to infer the less variability in historical loss rates, the more stable the line of coverage, and the greater degree of confidence in the loss projection. Also, the greater the volume of losses analyzed, the more stable the data and resulting projection. This selected loss rate is then applied to upcoming payroll to project losses for the upcoming policy year.

Actuarial Analyses. Many loss projections and actuarial studies include a confidence level analysis to assist the company in funding for a particular level of expected losses with some degree of certainty. Actuaries also review industry data and a company's own historical payout patterns to assist self-insured clients with potential investment strategies. Industry data in conjunction with a review of large losses also assist an actuary in recommending an appropriate level of risk retention. This information can be particularly valuable in structuring an excess insurance program and determining appropriate attachment points for specific and aggregate excess insurance.

While complete information is critical in evaluating the self-insurance option, the more subjective organizational and cultural issues should also be given weight in making the right judgement.

CHAPTER SEVEN:

Evaluating Alternative Risk Financing Plans

CHAPTER OVERVIEW: *Today, companies have a wide range of financing plans available for funding losses. These range from traditional insurance programs to some of the more sophisticated risk retention programs. Computer cash flow models are available to calculate after-tax, net present value costs associated with selected risk financing plans. In addition, it is important to consider the operational characteristics associated with alternative risk financing plans. Both qualitative and quantitative issues should factor into the selection of a risk financing program for any organization.*
In addition to qualified self-insurance, some plans commonly considered include guaranteed cost plans, incurred loss retros, paid loss retros, and large deductible plans.

Some plans offer a greater degree of budgeting certainty than others. While some companies are prepared to assume more administrative responsibilities, others simply do not have the staffing or the resources needed.

ONCE A CREDIBLE LOSS FORECAST HAS BEEN ESTABLISHED, THE NEXT STEP IS TO DETERMINE THE MOST EFFICIENT AND EFFECTIVE MEANS OF FUNDING THE PROJECTED LEVEL OF LOSSES. Again, this is an area where the experience and expertise of quality consulting professionals and advisors is valuable and warrants the investment. Careful attention should be devoted to identifying and comparing what appear to be viable financing plans based on the company's operating characteristics and financial goals. Cost estimates and program factors for each plan are obtained, and most brokers and consulting firms use sophisticated computer cash flow models to calculate the after-tax, net present value cost of each plan.

In addition, the operating characteristics associated with each plan are considered. Some plans offer a greater degree of budgeting certainty than others. While some companies are prepared to assume more administrative responsibilities, others find it more efficient and practical to outsource many administrative responsibilities. Some businesses feel they have senior management's support in instituting aggressive cost management strategies, thereby allowing them to retain higher levels of risk. In other instances, risk management may not yet have a strong commitment to controlling losses from senior management. It is not unusual for such operational considerations to overshadow the potential cost savings associated with the least expensive plan. Both qualitative and quantitative issues surrounding the plans and their potential ramifications for the company must be factored into the equation before a strong program recommendation can be made.

The Risk Financing Continuum

At one end of the spectrum are risk transfer plans or what are more commonly thought of as true insurance plans. At the opposite extreme are risk retention plans or what are typically referred to as self-insurance plans. Many plans exhibit elements of both risk transfer and risk retention and fall somewhere between the two points on the spectrum.

In general, risk financing plans can be viewed as extending along a continuum. At one end of the spectrum are risk transfer plans or what are more commonly thought of as true insurance plans. At the opposite extreme are risk retention plans or what are typically referred to as self-

RISK FINANCING CONTINUUM

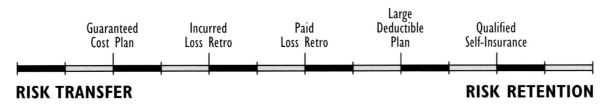

	Guaranteed Cost Plan	Incurred Loss Retro	Paid Loss Retro	Large Deductible Plan	Qualified Self-Insurance

RISK TRANSFER   **RISK RETENTION**

insurance plans. Many plans exhibit elements of both risk transfer and risk retention and fall somewhere between the two points on the spectrum. Various types of retrospectively-rated plans are good examples of plans exhibiting elements of both risk transfer and risk retention. These plans are loss sensitive up to a point at which time insurance is triggered and pays additional losses.

Some of the more common plans typically considered and evaluated in a self-insurance feasibility study include a guaranteed cost plan, an incurred loss retrospectively-rated plan, a paid loss retrospectively-rated plan, and a large deductible plan. Description highlights associated with these plans are provided below.

Guaranteed Cost Plans. A guaranteed cost plan is often considered one of the purest forms of insurance. An insured pays an insurance company an established premium, and in return the insurance company agrees to pay for all losses which arise during the policy year subject to policy conditions.

Premium is calculated based on the size of the company's operations and the types of exposure it represents. In the case of workers' compensation, industry rates are typically applied to an insured's payroll classifications to determine an insured's standard premium. An experience modification factor may be applied to reflect an insured's prior loss experience. Companies that have successfully controlled historical losses typically receive a premium credit while those suffering from rampant loss experience often must pay a premium surcharge.

One of the most prominent features of a guaranteed cost plan is that the premium is fixed for any given policy year. In other words, premium is not returned when losses are less than expected nor is additional premium collected when losses are more than anticipated. Because of the plan's static nature, some insureds become complacent about preventing and managing losses, even though unfavorable loss experience may be reflected in renewal premium rates.

One of the most prominent features of a guaranteed cost plan is that the premium is fixed for any given policy year.

Because the premium is established prior to the policy period, budgeting is made easy. Some guaranteed cost plans may be subject to audit, but a change in premium is only warranted by a change in exposure.

Another characteristic of the guaranteed cost plan is that it is typically accompanied by a service package. The insurance carrier provides all claims, loss control, and related account services. The bundling of services, as this is called, offers the advantage of simplicity but limits opportunities for the insured to have input on service program structure, authority levels, or the selection of medical and legal advisors. Bundled programs are more likely to reflect the culture of the insurer than that of the insured.

In recent years, many larger insureds have negotiated the right to contract for various elements of the services package from select providers.

Service Continuum

| Guaranteed Cost Plan | Incurred Loss Retro | Paid Loss Retro | Large Deductible Plan | Qualified Self-Insurance |

BUNDLED SERVICES   **UNBUNDLED SERVICES**

This approach, called the unbundling of services, allows insureds to retain many of the benefits associated with guaranteed cost plans while exercising greater control over the service delivery process.

A guaranteed cost plan offers very little in the way of cash flow benefits. Most guaranteed cost premiums are paid at policy inception or payments are spread over the course of the policy year. As a result, the insurance carrier retains use of and benefits from the loss reserves until claims and expenses are actually paid. On the other hand, the insured enjoys the benefit of a current year tax deduction as a result of premium payments.

Many companies embrace guaranteed cost plans because of the simplicity they offer and their attractive pricing in soft markets.

Incurred Loss Retro. An incurred loss retro is a loss sensitive insurance plan exhibiting elements of both risk transfer and risk retention.

Under an incurred loss retro, the insured pays the insurance carrier an initial premium, and this amount is later adjusted to reflect the insured's actual loss experience. If losses are less than expected, the insured may be due some return premium. If losses are more than expected, additional premium may be collected by the insurance company. Most incurred loss retros are characterized by a minimum and a maximum premium amount to limit potential swings in program costs.

Due to the loss sensitive nature of incurred loss retro plans, an insured is incentivized to prevent accidents and manage costs, which can have a very positive impact on long-term savings. An incurred loss retro also entitles an insured to all the services provided by the insurance carrier including safety, loss control, claims handling, and information reports.

Due to the loss sensitive nature of incurred loss retro plans, an insured is incentivized to prevent accidents and manage costs, which can have a very positive impact on long-term savings.

One of the drawbacks of an incurred loss retro is the uncertainty it introduces into the budgeting process. Not only can costs fluctuate during the current year as a result of varying losses, but fluctuations can occur in future years as a result of the retro adjustments. Also, incurred loss retros offer limited cash flow benefits since the insurance carrier retains control of the loss reserves.

Paid Loss Retro. A paid loss retro enables an insured to achieve some of the positive benefits associated with self-insurance without having to assume many of the responsibilities. Under a paid loss retro, the insured pays an initial premium deposit and establishes an escrow account from which losses are paid. The insurance company typically requires some form of security, such as a letter of credit or surety bond, for the difference between the initial premium deposit and the standard premium for the program. Over time, the security amount is adjusted as needed. Similarly, the insured adds additional funds to the escrow account on a periodic basis for claims payment purposes.

Like a self-insurance plan, a paid loss retro allows an insured to achieve substantial cash flow benefits since it is the insured who retains the loss reserves until claims payments are needed. There is also a strong incentive to control losses because of the loss sensitive nature of the plan.

While a paid loss retro resembles a self-insurance plan in terms of many of the benefits it has to offer, an insured is not subject to meeting and maintaining the extensive qualification and filing requirements associated with a self-insurance plan.

These two features, not having to qualify with the states and not having to build a service program, make a paid loss retro considerably easier to administer than a qualified self-insurance program. This could prove to be attractive for a company with multi-state exposures.

Moreover, the insured can capitalize upon the service package, corporate staff, and resources of an insurance company. These two features, not having to qualify with the states and not having to build a service program, make a paid loss retro considerably easier to administer than a qualified self-insurance program. This could prove to be attractive for a company with multi-state exposures.

Also, excess insurance is offered under a paid loss retro and certificates of insurance are issued as needed.

It should be noted, however, that the insured is still subject to residual market loadings and premium taxes. Also, an insurance carrier may be inclined to assess higher administrative charges under a paid loss retro than other types of plans as a result of losing the cash flow benefits and investment income opportunities.

Like other types of risk retention plans, the paid loss retro subjects the insured to a fairly high level of budgeting uncertainty as well as what could become pyramiding security requirements.

Large Deductible Plans. Another type of risk retention plan acceptable in many states for funding workers' compensation losses is the large deductible plan. This plan typically carries deductibles of $100,000 $250,000 or $500,000. The insured pays a substantially reduced premium due to the deductible feature. The insurance company pays all losses, including the deductible, and then bills the insured for reimbursement. Like many of the other risk retention plans, large deductibles typically require some type of surety bond, letter of credit, or other security instrument to secure payment of expected losses within the deductible.

Like a qualified self-insurance plan, the large deductible provides a strong incentive to control and manage losses and the insured enjoys significant cash flow benefits.

A large deductible plan shares many of the same characteristics as a paid loss retro in that premium taxes and related expenses are reduced substantially. In addition, the insured has access to the services of an insurance carrier, is not burdened with state filings and qualifications, and has access to certificates of insurance as needed for contractual purposes.

Like a qualified self-insurance plan, the large deductible provides a strong incentive to control and manage losses, and the insured enjoys significant cash flow benefits.

However, large deductibles are not an approved funding mechanism for workers' compensation losses in all states.

C HAPTER OVERVIEW: *Once the decision to become a qualified self-insurer is made, a detailed implementation plan should be developed. This plan should include contacting appropriate state authorities to discuss qualification requirements, designing and marketing an organization's excess insurance program, and the development of a comprehensive service plan conveying how the program will be administered and losses controlled. Because of the level of claims dollars at stake, the decision to self-administer versus the use of a third party administrator is one requiring utmost consideration.*

CHAPTER EIGHT:

Developing a Self-Insurance Implementation Plan

O NCE A COMPANY DECIDES TO SELF-INSURE ITS LOSSES, A COMPREHENSIVE AND WELL-DEFINED IMPLEMENTATION PLAN SHOULD BE DEVELOPED. Personnel and resources needed to establish and maintain the plan must be identified, and realistic timeframes for specific task completions should be communicated. A complete blueprint of the plan's operation should be developed to mitigate surprises and improve the program's chances for success.

A complete blueprint of the plan's operation should be developed to mitigate surprises and improve the program's chances for success.

Plan Fundamentals

Three specific areas needing immediate attention include: contacting and meeting with appropriate state authorities regarding a jurisdiction's specific rules, regulations, and required forms; developing an effective excess insurance program that reflects the self-insured's tolerance for risk; and designing a master service plan that details how the program will be administered, what services are needed and by whom they will be provided, and how the performance of the program will be measured.

State Regulation. First, many self-insured companies find it beneficial to meet and establish a relationship with state authorities. These individuals can serve as valuable informational resources, answer questions, and ensure the proper forms and filings are made. Most state regulatory authorities have experience with many self-insured organizations, and a self-insured candidate can benefit from their experience as well as gain a better understanding of the state's workers' compensation climate.

> *Most state regulatory authorities have experience with many self-insured organizations, and a self-insured candidate can benefit from their experience as well as gain a better understanding of the state's workers' compensation climate.*

Excess Insurance. A well-structured excess insurance program is an excellent means for self-insured organizations to cap their self-insured risk. Self-insureds should consider their financial circumstances, their cultural disposition toward risk, and market conditions for excess insurance in selecting levels of retention and limits of coverage. Moreover, many state authorities require some form of excess insurance as a part of the qualification process, and they often stipulate both the type of insurance and minimum limits of coverage required.

Plan Administration. Another area which must be defined is how the plan will be administered and who will provide the services.

Some companies elect to contract with outside vendors for program services, while others choose to provide services using internal staff. Many find a combination of resources best meets their needs. Both types of arrangements offer their own merits, and the true test becomes identifying the proper mix of internal and external resources based upon an organization's needs and characteristics. Understanding the issues surrounding self-administration versus the use of third party administrators can help a business make a more informed and profitable decision.

Self-Administration

Self-administration involves a company's decision to provide self-insurance program services using in-house resources. These include risk management information systems and services, safety and loss control, claims handling and investigation, check issuance, financial and accounting, actuarial, legal, and other management services deemed appropriate.

As a result, self-administration requires a tremendous commitment from management in terms of needed personnel and business resources. Qualified claims adjusters must be hired and licensed for the states in which they administer claims. Legal counsel must be provided in support of the self-insurance plan and a litigation plan must be developed. Trained safety engineers and loss control consultants are needed to ensure safe working conditions. Nursing professionals are sometimes hired to direct medical cost containment efforts with particular emphasis placed on catastrophic case management. All of these professionals must receive ongoing training to keep abreast of legislative developments and regulatory changes.

Additionally, appropriate work space and office materials must be provided. This includes telephone and communication systems and computer networking capabilities.

Reasons to Self-Administer. There are many reasons companies choose to self-administer their programs. Among the foremost is the desire to exert greater control over their programs. Driving this decision is the belief that they can achieve higher quality services at a lower cost than by contracting with outside firms. For example, they feel that by administering claims in-house they can positively impact claims outcomes, reduce the average cost of claims, improve employee relations, and save third party administration fees.

There are many reasons companies choose to self-administer their programs. Among the foremost is the desire to exert greater control over their programs.

By providing safety and loss control services in-house, these companies believe they can initiate a shift in corporate culture in such a way that management and employees will embrace safe work practices. An in-house safety engineer is generally perceived to have a strong vested interest in the company's loss control efforts.

The start-up of a self-insured, self-administered program is a huge undertaking. Some companies elect to move in this direction on a gradual basis and initially rely on the services and expertise of third party providers. Only after the program is established do they choose to bring services in-house. This approach helps mitigate some of the risk and enables the company to define the proper program approach over time.

Reasons Not to Self-Administer. There are many reasons companies elect not to self-administer their programs. Instead, they rely on outside service providers to support the program. For a company with a multi-state self-insured program, one of the primary reasons not to self-administer the program is the tremendous effort it takes for staff to remain current on legislative, legal and regulatory matters among the states. State licenses must also be maintained. Training becomes an onerous, time-consuming and expensive task. In addition, staff must stay abreast of new products and services in the marketplace. A self-administered company must also manage turnover and have immediate staff replacements when sudden vacancies arise.

For a company with a multi-state self-insured program, one of the primary reasons not to self-administer the program is the tremendous effort it takes for staff to remain current on legislative, legal and regulatory matters among the states.

Another challenge becomes convincing insurance carriers of a company's ability to self-administer a program effectively. The insurance company may not perceive a self-insured employer whose core business is not claims administration to have the same quality as a third party administrator. As a result, a self-administered company may be limited in its choice of excess carriers. The level of risk retention or type of coverage a self-administered company is forced to accept may pose a higher risk or expense than originally anticipated.

Self-administered companies must also be prepared to handle claims in remote locations as well as address what some companies experience in seasonal demands in claims. These factors can erode what was originally perceived to be potential program savings. Also, a self-administered program can strain employee relations if the workforce perceives resources are not directed at maintaining a safe working environment or that claims are not handled fairly.

Because of the sophisticated systems and complex procedures which must be developed, a self-administered program requires a long-term commitment. Also, with greater control comes greater responsibility. Credit for success or blame for failure rests internally.

Working With a Third Party Administrator. With so much on the line, a number of self-insured companies choose to purchase services from third party providers. For many, an unbundled approach to services allows them to capitalize upon the introduction of new products and services and quickly take advantage of new regulatory or market developments. Corporate staff remains lean. Specialized resources can be identified and employed to address high dollar situations.

For many, an unbundled approach to services allows them to capitalize upon the introduction of new products and services and quickly take advantage of new regulatory or market developments.

Like a traditional insurance program, a self-insurance program requires risk management information systems and services, safety and loss control, claims handling and investigation, financial and accounting, actuarial, legal, and other desired services. The key to success becomes hiring qualified providers who understand a company's particular needs and actively managing the provision of services on an ongoing basis.

Selecting a Third Party Administrator. One of the first tasks which must be accomplished is to readily identify the services needed for a successful program. This effort must be directed by the self-insured with assistance from brokers, risk consultants or other program partners as needed. For example, a self-insured must address what type of claims reporting best suits its needs. Some organizations have computers at every workstation making electronic claims reporting a viable option. In other instances, the workforce does not possess computer skills or language barriers may be present causing a company to examine some of the more traditional reporting options such as telephonic reporting, faxing, or mailing the reports.

Once services are defined, complete service specifications should be developed and presented to qualified vendors in the marketplace.

Once services are defined, complete service specifications should be developed and presented to qualified vendors in the marketplace. The identification and selection of program partners is a significant undertaking, and the outcome can have a tremendous impact on a program's future success.

Planning is crucial and vendors must be allowed adequate time to respond to the request for proposal.

Planning is crucial and vendors must be allowed adequate time to respond to the request for proposal. Also, once written proposals are received, extensive effort should be poured into the review and comparison of competing providers' bids. Some key questions to ask include: Did the written response conform to the original service specifications? Did the proposal reflect an understanding of my business? Has the vendor demonstrated an ability to handle the scope and complexity of my claims? Did the proposal contain references from similar size companies? And most importantly, will it achieve program goals?

As a part of this evaluation process, present and former client references should be contacted. Look at the types of references provided and how they reflect a particular company's corresponding needs. Ask the tough questions relating to service, professionalism, and length of relationship. Do the client references project enthusiasm for a particular vendor's services and what kinds of success stories can they share? When problems arose, how were they handled?

Based on a review of written proposals and discussions with client references, narrow the list of candidate providers to a few finalists with whom to schedule both service site visits and oral presentations. Ask to visit sites that reflect the service model under consideration. Insist that members of the proposed service team participate in the oral presentations. Look for confirmation that the candidate providers can actually deliver the services being promised. Who best understands and will be able to communicate the client's service philosophy? Which team can more readily respond to new challenges that might arise over the course of the program?

Key Selection Criteria

While exact specifications will vary, several key criteria which a self-insured should consider include:

Qualifications of staff. Who will be the primary contact person? What is the experience level of the team and how long have they been with this particular firm? What education and professional credentials does the team have to offer? What is the average workload of the team members?

Key Selection Criteria:

- Qualifications of staff
- Valued expertise
- Company qualifications
- Depth of resources
- Ancillary services
- Price

Valued Expertise. Does the firm have expertise in your specific industry or similar types of companies? In the case of a qualified self-insurance program, what percentage of the firm's business is workers' compensation related?

Company Qualifications. How long has the company been in business? Can the company provide appropriate information on its financial status? What are the firm's plans for future expansion? Are the firm's professionals properly licensed to perform the desired services? What is the firm's retention rate of employees and clients? What is the firm's client mix?

Depth of Resources. Does the candidate firm have the depth of resources to recognize and address new opportunities or changes in program requirements?

Ancillary Services. What ancillary services does the firm have to offer? Does the firm offer its services on an unbundled basis?

Price. How does the pricing among service providers compare? Do they offer performance-based incentive guarantees?

A successful implementation of a new program requires careful planning. A transition program should address such elements as data processing, data conversion, and communicating with supervisors and employees.

The identification and selection of third party providers is a considerable undertaking and one that will have a significant impact upon the outcome of the program. The performance of program partners often makes the difference between a self-insurance program's success and a program's failure.

CHAPTER NINE:

Managing a Self-Insurance Program

CHAPTER OVERVIEW: *A successful qualified self-insurance program requires a high level of involvement on the part of the self-insured. The program must be effectively managed if intended benefits are to be achieved. Some key management activities include defining service needs, understanding partner capabilities, keeping informed of regulatory developments, communicating expectations to others within the organization, promoting success stories and the actions of those who have helped prevent accidents and control costs, and making continuous adjustments within the program. Whatever the business climate today, the organization is likely to face a very different set of circumstances tomorrow. The ability to anticipate change and respond accordingly is a key corporate attribute essential to effective risk management.*

MAKING THE DECISION TO SELF-INSURE AND IMPLEMENTING THE PROGRAM ARE ONLY THE BEGINNING OF A LONG JOURNEY. It is, however, a road which can lead to sizeable cost savings and significant program improvements. Active management and ongoing involvement are key to a newly established program's long-term success.

Steps to Managing a Self-Insurance Program

There are several steps a self-insured company can take to ensure effective management of the program. These include: defining service needs, understanding partner capabilities, keeping informed of regulatory developments, communicating expectations within the organization, promoting success stories, and making continuous adjustments.

Defining Service Needs. One of the most profitable investments a self-insured company can make is taking time to identify, understand and communicate its service needs. Each company is different in its operations, workforce, product and service offerings, geographical locations, corporate philosophy, and long-term goals.

Steps to Managing a Self-Insurance Program:

- Define service needs
- Understand partner capabilities
- Keep informed of regulatory developments
- Communicate expectations within the organization
- Promote success stories
- Make continuous adjustments

For example, hospital employees may be very different from workers at a truck manufacturer. Yet both organizations must offer a safe work environment and be responsive to accidents when they occur. The approach to achieve these goals within the organizations is very different.

The development of complete service specifications is invaluable but often overlooked as many companies settle for a "one size fits all" approach to service procurement. Moreover, service needs will change over time as a company evolves. Continual monitoring of service needs is essential.

Understanding Partner Capabilities. A second key to effective management is getting to know a provider's service capabilities and establishing a true partnership with the service team. Many service vendors offer specialized services over and above the basic service package. Some of these services are available to the self-insured simply for the asking or at a nominal service fee. An example is having a well-trained safety engineer conduct a specialized training program on how to prevent slips and falls, how to address a company's blood-bourne pathogen exposure, or how to reduce carpal tunnel and other repetitive motion injuries. Alternatively, providers may offer their library of training materials and videos to clients at no charge.

It pays to get to know the experts and capitalize upon their experience. Also, take interest in a provider's research and development efforts.

It pays to get to know the experts and capitalize upon their experience. Also, take interest in a provider's research and development efforts.

Monitoring Regulatory Developments. Third, keep abreast of regulatory developments. Get to know individuals within the various state agencies. They offer a wealth of experience as it pertains to self-insurance programs. Establish channels of communication to ensure the organization is aware of regulatory changes and developments.

Also, self-insureds should work with their legal counsel to keep informed of various court cases and rulings that could have implications for their programs. For example, keep abreast of tax rulings which could have implications as to when program expenses can be deducted or case rulings pertaining to a claimant's circumstances and settlement outcome. Be active and lobby for improvements to the self-insurance process in the various states.

Communicating Expectations. Fourth, communicate risk management's expectations of others within the organization. A successful self-insurance program requires a complete organizational effort. People at various levels and within various departments must understand what is expected of them in order to achieve success. This includes senior managers who must lend full philosophical and financial support to the program as well as the assembly line workers who must adhere to safety practices. Increased communication is an essential part of any self-insurance program.

Promoting Success Stories. Promote successes within the organization and their impact on the self-insurance program. Applaud departments who set new records for incident free workdays. Recognize supervisors who achieve twenty-four hour claims reporting standards. Congratulate the injured employee for an expeditious return to work. Positive promotions are excellent means to raise the visibility and stature of any program.

A successful self-insurance program requires a complete organizational effort. People at various levels and within various departments must understand what is expected of them in order to achieve success.

Many self-insured companies find cost allocation programs can benefit their program results substantially. In general, cost allocation programs dictate that the location or department incurring the loss pay all or a portion of the related expenses. These types of programs serve as strong incentives to prevent and manage losses and are often reflective of a company's culture. But successful cost allocation programs must be communicated, and people within the organization must understand the mechanics of how such a program works.

Making Continuous Program Improvements. Make continuous improvements in the program. Most successful companies are dynamic by nature and successful self-insurance programs must exhibit this same quality. Self-insurers' needs will change on a continual basis.

While some businesses are aggressively pursuing merger and acquisition opportunities, others are managing corporate downsizing. Corporate research and development efforts spawn the introduction of new products and services in the marketplace. A workplace catastrophe involving ten fatalities may produce unwanted press coverage and media attention. The number of people in the risk management department may be reduced by half. The company's stock price may soar, increasing the organization's attractiveness to investors in the financial marketplace.

Most successful companies are dynamic by nature and successful self-insurance programs must exhibit this same quality.

Each of these circumstances can have significant ramifications for a self-insurance program. In some cases, the claims management strategy should be redefined, the risk retention level should be increased, or contract renegotiations with vendors should occur. Whatever the business circumstances today, chances are a very different set of corporate challenges will arise tomorrow. The ability to change is essential and is one of the most valuable characteristics of a well-managed self-insurance program.

CHAPTER TEN:

Establishing a Strong Safety Culture

CHAPTER OVERVIEW: Because of the loss sensitive nature of a qualified self-insurance program, a strong safety and loss prevention program is essential. Safe work practices must go far beyond written rules and procedures and actually become a way of life for employees at the workplace. The development of a strong safety culture will serve to protect an organization's financial interests and employee investment. Common characteristics found among strong safety and loss control programs include: senior management commitment and involvement in the program, comprehensive education and training, and receptiveness to employee input and suggestions.

AN EFFECTIVE SAFETY AND LOSS CONTROL PROGRAM CAN PAY BIG DIVIDENDS IN TERMS OF REDUCED PROGRAM COSTS. The importance of safety and loss control becomes even more pronounced in a self-insurance program where program costs are driven by losses. To the extent such losses can be prevented or contained, success can be achieved.

Values of the Safety Culture

Two of the most obvious and compelling objectives in any organization are the protection of financial assets and the preservation of the lives and well-being of employees.

Protecting Financial Assets. Safety and loss control are best known as means of financial protection. A successful program will reduce both direct and indirect costs. Direct costs are the hard dollar costs associated with claims such as medical costs, lost time wages and legal fees. Indirect costs are less apparent and as a result, their impact is often underestimated. Indirect costs include the costs associated with the additional administrative tasks and completion of paperwork following a claim, reduced productivity as fellow employees become distracted during the course of a workplace accident, and the additional time needed for training replacement workers to perform the newly assigned tasks. Safety and loss control are aimed directly at preventing and controlling these expenses.

Protecting Human Life and Well-Being. Successful organizations are those that achieve and maintain high levels of production on an ongoing basis. Each year businesses spend significant dollars to attract and retain quality employees. The value of an organization's workforce cannot be overstated. Skilled and productive employees who are not hampered by workplace injuries or illnesses are what drive an organization's production standards. Safety and loss control programs are aimed directly at protecting the employees and maintaining their quality of life.

Skilled and productive employees who are not hampered by workplace injuries or illnesses are what drive an organization's production standards.

Critical Safety and Loss Control Program Characteristics

Safety and loss control programs will vary depending upon a company's operational exposures, workforce characteristics, and historical accident patterns. However, most successful programs share some common characteristics including a strong management

Examples of Direct and Indirect Costs

Direct Costs:
- Medical costs
- Lost time wages
- Legal fees

Indirect Costs:
- Additional administration
- Reduced productivity
- Temporary replacements

commitment to safety and loss control principles, a comprehensive education and training program, and genuine receptiveness to employee input and suggestions.

Management Commitment. Like most successful corporate initiatives, a successful safety and loss control program requires a strong commitment from senior management. Executives must understand the value of safety and loss control practices and completely embrace loss prevention as an important operational initiative.

Executives must understand the value of safety and loss control practices and completely embrace loss prevention as an important operational initiative.

Whether a company is developing a new safety and loss control program or renewing its commitment to an existing plan, senior management should communicate the company's safety policy. Employees need to understand that the company is committed to providing a safe work environment.

Senior managers should also communicate the company's safety goals and objectives. These goals should be both realistic and measurable. For example, an organizational objective could be to reduce the number of carpal tunnel injuries by 50% over the next twelve months, conduct quarterly educational and training programs for all employees, or reduce the number of lost workdays by 25% during the upcoming policy year.

Senior management should also establish a system of accountability. Just as managers are held accountable for meeting production and sales goals, they need to be held accountable for workplace safety. When safe work practices are ignored, organizations often pay severe financial consequences in terms of higher losses. In cases of gross negligence, senior management and board members may be held criminally liable for unsafe working conditions. This can be costly to a company and dangerous for its employees.

Senior management should also lend financial support to the safety and loss control program. It takes financial resources to develop a comprehensive education and training program. Likewise, it takes resources to ensure equipment and machinery are properly maintained. Worn out pieces should be retired and new equipment and machinery purchases should be made. Personal protective equipment must be purchased and provided to all employees.

Finally, senior managers must lend support to the program by way of example. They, too, must follow posted warnings and wear protective gear as required. Ongoing, active interest is essential.

When safe work practices are ignored, organizations often pay severe financial consequences in terms of higher losses. This can be costly to a self-insured company and dangerous for its employees.

Education and Training. Another element common to effective safety and loss control programs is comprehensive education and training. These efforts begin on day one when a new employee is hired and continue throughout the course of employment. A complete orientation program should clearly state the company's safety policy and expectations, followed by individual instructions as to how to perform the job safely. Periodic updates to ensure top of the mind awareness should be a part of the training initiative.

Advancements in communication and technology offer companies many ways to deliver their safety message. These range from printed materials to digital video productions to web-based or interactive CD presentations. Alternative media can complement a company's personal instruction.

Also, some third party administrators and program partners can be valuable resources in the training and communication efforts. Many offer well-designed materials to enhance the communication process and ensure a smooth implementation of the program.

Although corporate philosophies vary, many organizations use incentive programs and reward systems to recognize safe behavior. Some of the programs take the form of games such as safety bingo or contests to determine which department can go the longest accident free. Rewards might include company apparel and gear, cash incentives, or additional vacation days.

Clearly, employees who perform tasks each and every day are real experts when it comes to identifying safe work practices. Successful organizations know how to capitalize upon this vast knowledge and resource base.

Employee Input and Suggestions. A third element common to effective safety and loss control programs is genuine receptiveness to employee input and suggestions. Clearly, employees who perform tasks each and every day are real experts when it comes to identifying safe work practices. Successful organizations know how to capitalize upon this vast knowledge and resource base. These organizations have created an environment in which employees are motivated and feel comfortable sharing safety related ideas. Some organizations offer financial awards to employees whose ideas are successfully implemented. Moreover, these suggestions are reviewed and implemented whenever possible.

In order to formalize the process, many organizations establish safety committees. These committees generally consist of three to seven people at a given location. The group is charged with identifying, promoting, and enforcing safe work practices. Safety committees typically meet at established times and places throughout the year. Minutes from the meetings are recorded and distributed to managers and supervisors.

Safety committees are also responsible for accident review and investigations. Their objective is not to point fingers but to determine the underlying cause and how to prevent future occurrences.

Committee members also perform location inspections on an ongoing basis to identify unsafe acts or unsafe conditions. They are responsible for promoting awareness and can serve as an excellent liaison between employees and management when it comes to safety issues.

Safety Committee Responsibilities

- Review and investigate accidents
- Perform location inspections
- Promote safety awareness
- Facilitate communication between management and employees

Committees tend to be most effective when they are comprised of members from different departments and at different levels within the organization. Most committee positions are subject to rotation to ensure the group remains dynamic in its thinking. It is important that management demonstrate full support for the efforts of the safety committee.

In addition, organizations are well advised to identify a safety champion. This person may be appointed a full-time safety director who is charged with ensuring the safety and loss control program's success. In other instances, this person may be someone who understands and recognizes the value of safety and agrees to assume this added responsibility as part of an existing role. This individual must be well respected and have a good understanding of the company's operations. Another key characteristic is the ability to understand and act upon loss trends and statistics. This person should also possess the ability to instigate change in both attitudes and behavior.

CHAPTER ELEVEN

Streamlining the Claims Management Process

Cｈａｐｔｅｒ Oｖｅｒｖｉｅｗ: *Claims payments account for most of the costs of a qualified self-insurance program. Quality claims service is essential. To achieve the level of quality claims services needed for a successful program, a self-insured should define the internal claims process, establish standards of performance for the claims administrator, and perform comprehensive audits of the entire process including the review of selected files. Some progressive claims administrators offer negotiated performance guarantees as an effective tool for assuring high levels of performance. The development of a quality claims program is an investment with potentially high rewards.*

Cｌｅａｒｌｙ, ｔｈｅ ｍａｊｏｒｉｔｙ ｏｆ ｅｘｐｅｎｓｅ ａｓｓｏｃｉａｔｅｄ ｗｉｔｈ ａ ｓｅｌｆ-ｉｎｓｕｒａｎｃｅ ｐｒｏｇｒａｍ ｉｓ ｉｎ ｃｌａｉｍｓ ｃｏｓｔｓ. As a result, the programs and procedures that address what happens immediately following an accident are largely responsible for a self-insurance program's success or failure. Whether a firm elects to self-administer claims or contracts with a third party administrator to provide claims services, the quality of work performed must be high. In order to achieve quality claims services, a self-insured company is advised to define the claims process, establish standards of performance for the claims administrator, and audit the claims process and quality of services provided.

Defining the Claims Process

The first step a self-insured must undertake is to clearly define the claims process. What happens immediately following an accident? Instructions need to be in place to ensure the injured party receives immediate medical treatment. In some instances, this consists of minor first aid treatment on site, while more severe injuries require that the injured employee be transported to a nearby medical facility or hospital. Under ideal circumstances, the supervisor will accompany the injured employee to the doctor's office.

There should also be clear instructions as to which physicians or medical facilities should provide treatment. In some states employees can see their physician of choice while other states allow the employer to direct medical care. Most successful programs utilize the services of preferred providers. Many of these preferred provider organizations offer specialized occupational health services as well as provide negotiated discounts to member companies. The emphasis should be placed on providing quality care that allows the self-insured company to exert control over the medical treatment process.

Once an injured employee's medical needs are addressed, attention should be turned to investigating the accident. What were the underlying causes of the accident and how can future mishaps be prevented? Interview other employees who witnessed the accident. Investigate the scene. Much of this information may be useful to the claims adjuster in handling the case.

Also, it is critical that the employer complete the necessary first report of injury and contact the claims administrator as soon as possible. Electronic reporting or 1-800 telephonic reporting are expedient means of communication. The sooner the claims administrator knows about the accident, the sooner the claims process can be initiated and an adjuster can follow up with both the injured employee and treating physician. Early reporting of claims is one of the most effective strategies a business can employ for controlling claims costs.

The Role of the Supervisor

- Obtain medical treatment for injured employee
- Investigate the accident and determine cause
- Report the claim to the administrator
- Follow-up with injured employee
- Integrate injured employee into return to work program
- Assist injured employee until recovery is achieved

The severity of the injury and the quality of medical and rehabilitation services will determine how long an employee is off work. During this time, the self-insured should maintain ongoing communications with the employee concerning recovery and progress. Many companies take the extra means to express care and concern for the injured employee during this time of uncertainty by offering family assistance, sending cards or flowers, and ensuring payments are made on a timely basis. If employers do not do these things, the injured employee may seek attorney involvement. Employee uncertainty is one of the leading causes of attorney representation.

Early return to work programs have also been shown to reduce claims costs. While many injured employees are not able to return to their original positions immediately, most are able to perform some tasks with certain restrictions. This type of position tends to speed the recovery process and encourage employees to stay active at the workplace.

For example, an employee with a broken foot cannot continue to carry twenty-five pound boxes to the loading dock but could assist elsewhere in the plant with the box labeling function.

In addition to defining the steps to be taken following an accident, the self-insured must educate its employees as to how the claims process should work. Employees must understand they are to report accidents to their supervisor immediately. Supervisors must ensure proper medical care is administered, complete the necessary paperwork, and investigate the causes at the accident scene. Location managers, department supervisors, and front line workers must understand and embrace a return to work philosophy and know what is expected if such a program is to be successful. The goal of any claims management program should be the safe and speedy recovery of every injured employee.

Examples of Performance Standards

- Regular claimant contact
- Timely benefit payments
- Medical bill audits
- Excess carrier notification
- Communication of severe claims
- Evaluation of subrogation
- Educational seminars
- Maximum case loads

Establishing Standards of Performance

A second step toward ensuring a successful claims management program is establishing standards of performance for the claims administrator. These standards of performance should be reflective of the internal claims process and an assessment of the company's overall claims needs.

For example, the self-insured may specify the injured employee and treating physician be contacted within twenty-four hours of receiving the initial claims notice. Examples of other performance standards include: contacting claimants at defined intervals, making indemnity benefit payments on a timely basis, auditing medical bills, notifying the excess carrier as needed, contacting the employer when a claim reserve reaches a specified amount, evaluating subrogation opportunities on all claims, and conducting at least one educational seminar over the course of the year. A self-insured might also specify levels of professional qualification for adjusters handling certain types of claims and define maximum permissible caseloads.

The development of performance standards will be varied and limited only by imagination and good judgement. The true test is identifying those actions having the greatest impact on the claims process and resulting outcome.

Negotiating Performance Guarantees

Some companies are taking the development of performance standards to the next level and negotiating performance

Common Types of Performance Guarantees
- Implementation
- Process
- Results

guarantees with third party providers, especially third party claims administrators.

Performance guarantees are built around incentive compensation arrangements. They are typically structured in such a way that the service provider puts a percentage of its fee at risk if certain criteria are not met and/or shares a percentage of savings if costs are reduced or other goals are achieved.

Three of the most common types of performance guarantee arrangements are based upon an effective implementation, compliance with the process, and achieving results. An implementation-driven performance guarantee focuses on such functions as data conversion, file reviews within a defined timeframe, or the development of a communications and implementation plan. Process-driven performance guarantees center on compliance with service instructions and adherence to service standards. This might include twenty-four hour claimant contact, timely payment of benefits, or compliance with statutory requirements. Results-driven performance guarantees focus on the achievement of such measures as a reduction in disability duration, reduction in annual paid losses, increased preferred provider utilization rates, or a reduction in average claims costs. These types of agreements have produced positive results for both clients and providers because they require both parties to clearly define and communicate service expectations and program capabilities.

Performing a Claims Audit

A third component essential to a successful claims program is the performance of comprehensive claims program audits. This is a natural outcome if the claims process has been clearly defined and service standards have been developed and agreed upon by the claims administrator. The claims process should be reviewed in detail, findings documented, and adjustments made as needed. Similarly, actual claims files should be reviewed to ensure they reflect the performance of established service standards. Claims adjusters and supervisors should be interviewed to identify and address potential problem areas. Loss reserves should be evaluated to determine if they are reasonable and appropriate. Some self-insureds recognize and reward superior performance by individual claims adjusters.

A successful claims management program requires a high degree of active involvement on the part of the self-insured. However, given the amount of dollars at stake, it is an investment with potentially high rewards.

CHAPTER TWELVE:

Analyzing Risk Management Data and Information

CHAPTER OVERVIEW: *Complete and accurate information is important to every phase of a self-insurance plan. It is used in developing safety and loss prevention measures, designing claims management strategies, and making administrative and financing decisions. In evaluating and measuring program performance, self-insureds often look to both internal and external sources of program information and loss data. Both can be valuable in determining what adjustments to make and where to direct resources. This ongoing need for information makes the development or selection of a risk management information system a key component of a well-run program.*

INFORMATION IS IMPORTANT TO MANAGING SAFETY AND LOSS CONTROL, ESTABLISHING CLAIMS HANDLING STRATEGIES, AND CONTROLLING PROGRAM COSTS. To ensure a self-insurance program's long-term success, it is important to measure performance. Ideally, benchmarks or baseline measures of performance should be established at the onset of the program. These standards of measurement can be based upon both internal data comparisons and external industry statistics. Many companies also find it useful to establish service standards and then measure adherence to these standards of performance.

Evaluating Internal Data and Information

On an internal basis, track loss information diligently. Compare historical losses and number of claims. It is helpful to develop and trend historical losses and payrolls to calculate loss rates for prior policy years. This type of comparison enables a company to consider the effects of a 35% increase in losses versus a 20% reduction in payroll. Similarly, it is helpful to review claims trends. Again, a comparison of historical claims to historical payrolls can account for any significant increases or decreases in exposure.

Also, it will be useful for most employers to track losses, claims, and payrolls on a per state basis. Does the volume of claims justify maintaining a self-insurance program in a particular state? Are claims costs reported in a particular state exceptionally high? Is this a reflection of the regulatory climate in that state?

It is important to help location managers understand the implications of both direct and indirect costs and how these costs relate to additional production and sales revenues.

Another useful measurement involves comparing losses among the various facilities. Recognizing differences in the size and type of exposure, how does one group's performance compare to another? What is the average claim amount and incident rate within each of the facilities? An exceptionally high incident rate at one facility may be reflective of an apathetic management team. Alternatively, management may be focused solely on production issues with little regard for safety. It is important to help location managers understand the implications of both direct and indirect costs and how these costs relate to additional production and sales revenues. Taking this process a step further, examine how the losses and incident rates compare among the various departments within a given facility.

The advantage to making internal comparisons of data is that a company can ensure valid comparisons are being made. Losses can be developed and trended using accepted actuarial principles and techniques. Companies can be sure the data is clean and be certain what cost components are included in cost summaries.

Also, analyze losses according to the types of injuries occurring. This information is valuable in developing safety and loss control programs and procedures. Resources can be aimed at those areas generating the

Resources can be aimed at those areas generating the highest number of incidents to achieve a more immediate and sizeable reduction in claims costs.

highest number of incidents to achieve a more immediate and sizeable reduction in claims costs. For example, back injuries may account for the majority of claims costs, indicating the need for improved training programs or better hiring and placement practices. An exceptionally high number of eye injuries may indicate the need for purchasing safety glasses or enforcing the rule that the glasses be worn at all times. A high number of slips and falls may point to the need for protective footwear or slip resistant flooring.

An employer should also look at incident characteristics. Are there an unusually high number of incidents reported at the beginning of the holiday season? Are Monday morning injuries the result of a weekend recreational softball tournament gone awry? The data hold innumerable answers and over time the ability to read between the lines and look behind the numbers and statistics becomes a valuable skill.

Evaluating External Data and Information

Another type of analysis involves comparing losses and claims data to industry statistics. Statistics may be obtained from such organizations and agencies as the U.S Bureau of Labor Statistics, National Council on Compensation Insurance, National Safety Council, Workers' Compensation Research Institute, or private consulting firms.

Types of data which may be obtained include: claims per 100 employees, lost workdays per 100 employees, average medical cost and average indemnity cost per claim, program costs as a percentage of payroll, and program costs compared to product costs.

It is interesting for a firm in a particular industry to measure its program performance against the performance of competing firms in the same industry. It is imperative, however, to ensure that comparable data is used in making comparisons. For example, are losses developed to their estimated ultimate value? Have the losses been trended to reflect changes in medical inflation and benefit changes among the various states? Have losses been limited to a certain dollar amount before being included in the total? A large $250,000 loss can skew a loss total significantly and mask an otherwise successful year in terms of incident reductions. How do external firms define claims? Do the claims totals include medical only claims? Do the claims totals include all incidents reported including near misses? Including all incident rates can skew a frequency rate significantly and lead to an inaccurate comparison.

Industry associations are a good source for this type of data. Examples are the National Restaurant Association and the National Retailers Association.

While program comparisons to external industry data can be insightful, the importance of internal data comparisons cannot be overlooked. A company must measure its own performance against historical patterns to determine the effectiveness of cost reduction programs put in place and to determine how best to expend limited resources to achieve maximum program results.

Information Needs and Uses

Information is important in developing a company's claims initiative. For example, what is the average cost of medical claims versus the average cost of indemnity claims? Does the ratio of medical expenses to indemnity costs seem reasonable? How many claims require first aid treatment? What percentage of injured employees are using preferred providers for medical treatment? What percentage of claims are being litigated? Is there a particular attorney who is representing a high number of a self-insured's cases? What is the average length of time an injured worker is away from the workplace? What percentage of injured employees are participating in return to work programs? What is the average length of stay in a light duty program? Which locations are not using return to work programs? A self-insured should identify the information most useful to its claims management program and track it over time.

Information is also used for financial management purposes. Self-insurance programs may experience a higher degree of uncertainty and greater fluctuation in costs than fully-insured plans, but steps can be taken to avoid financial surprises.

Key Data Points:

- Claims and Loss Summaries
- Costs by Location
- Types of Injuries
- Medical to Indemnity Ratio
- Litigation Rates
- Disability Duration
- PPO Utilization
- Return to Work Participation

Actuarial analyses are valuable to ensure a program is properly funded. Actuaries can help determine the proper level of loss reserves a company should have on hand. Similarly, actuaries can assess a company's historical losses to make a projection of losses for the upcoming policy year. This estimate can be valuable for budgeting purposes. Actuaries can also examine loss payout patterns, and the resulting information may be useful as a company considers its investment options. While it is not necessary for a self-insured to master the performance of actuarial techniques, it is helpful to understand the results of the analyses and be able to communicate these results and the rationale behind them effectively to senior management.

Selecting a Risk Management Information System

Because of the information requirements associated with a self-insurance program, a risk management information system is vital. A well-designed system can be a valuable asset to the program. Such a system is particularly critical for programs that experience high claims volumes or have frequent electronic reporting requirements. Some companies have the technological expertise in-house to design a system to capture the needed information, while others find it more cost effective to purchase an existing system from an information systems provider. Also, many third party administrators offer the option of systems with full capabilities including analyzing, reporting and tracking claims data. These systems alleviate the problems of having to develop, acquire or maintain an in-house system. Many systems on the market today can be customized to address a company's specific needs.

Ownership of data is another key consideration regardless of whether a self-insured is purchasing risk management information system services from a third party administrator or building an internal system. A self-insured is well-advised to ensure that it retains ownership of the data.

 In evaluating system capabilities, an employer should remember that information and reporting packages need to be developed to serve multiple stakeholders within an organization. For example, data should be presented in a way that accommodates the needs of operational, risk management, and senior management staff.

At the operational and risk management levels, reports should address the program in detail. Graphics that provide both the current status of losses as well as historical loss trends are useful. These should be prepared for the overall company level as well as the operating unit level. Ideally, the reports will address key program measures for claims volumes, closing rates, and incurred and paid amounts. They should also help identify the cost drivers in the program.

When available, the report should also include benchmark data. This might be based on the administrator's overall data, common industry data, or Standard Industrial Classifications (SIC).

At the senior management level, a one-page "dashboard" document is an excellent way to communicate the program's status quickly and easily. These reports typically compare the current program status to either targets or past period performance. They generally address eight to twelve critical success factors. It is an effective way to provide senior executives with an indication of trends and a brief analysis of the major factors contributing to the program's current status.

With the advancement of technology, the whole area of metrics and benchmarking will likely continue to grow giving employers powerful information tools and enhanced decision making capabilities. Employers should be able to anticipate and clearly define their organization's information needs. It is important to develop specifications and take time to understand a system's complete capabilities. Some risk information systems now offer web-based access to claims data. Because so many facets of the program rely on accurate information to make informed decisions, a good information system is a key investment.

CHAPTER THIRTEEN

CHAPTER OVERVIEW: *Each year businesses pour extensive investments into the development of sophisticated cost management programs. A strong communications program is what enables organizations to capitalize upon these investments. People throughout the company need to know what their roles and responsibilities are and how their actions impact the overall performance of the plan. Many of the same marketing and sales techniques used to promote corporate products and services are being used to develop strong risk management communications plans.*

Launching a Successful Communications Campaign

STRONG COMMUNICATION IS AN INTEGRAL PART OF A SUCCESSFUL SELF-INSURANCE PROGRAM. People within a self-insured organization must understand their roles and responsibilities and how their actions impact the program's performance.

Businesses spend thousands of dollars developing program protocols and procedures aimed at preventing and controlling losses. They are meaningless unless people within the company are aware of their existence, understand what is expected of them, and comply with the programs and guidelines which have been established.

For example, a well-written safety and loss control manual is useless if safe work practices are not taught and reinforced in the workplace everyday. A twenty-four hour claims reporting standard is ineffective in a business which experiences a high level of turnover if incoming managers are not trained on telephone reporting procedures. A widespread preferred provider organization network offers little value to a company if employees are unaware of the participating physicians, their locations, and the benefits of seeking in-network treatment. Personal protective equipment simply clutters the job site if it is not properly used and rules for its usage are not consistently enforced. Communication is the mechanism which enables self-insured companies to capitalize upon their investments in these types of cost management programs.

Risk Management Communications Challenges

There are many challenges to developing and implementing a successful risk management communications program. These must be understood and overcome if a communications initiative is to be successful. Some of the more common hurdles include: misconceptions surrounding workers' compensation; the technical nature of the information to be communicated; and the information overload facing modern workers.

First, a successful communications plan must take into account existing misconceptions about workers' compensation. These misconceptions often result in irrational actions at the workplace and drive workers' compensation costs up. For example, some managers abide by the

Businesses spend thousands of dollars developing program protocols and procedures aimed at preventing and controlling losses. They are meaningless unless people within the company are aware of their existence, understand what is expected of them, and comply with the programs and guidelines which have been established.

philosophy that production goals must be met at all costs with little regard for safety measures. Some supervisors act as if all workers' compensation claims are fraudulent and do not respond to injured workers with the care and compassion which is needed. Some employees believe they must prove they were not at fault and seek legal counsel in order to obtain benefits. These types of misunderstandings only serve to reiterate the need for ongoing and consistent risk management communications.

A successful communications plan must take into account existing misconceptions about workers' compensation. These misconceptions often result in irrational actions at the workplace and drive workers' compensation costs up.

Second, much of the information which must be communicated is technical and complex. For example, risk managers must explain such actuarial concepts as loss development and trending when it comes to preparing sound financial statements; excess insurance policy language when it comes to discussing exposure assessments; and legal strategies and objectives when it comes to protecting a company's image in the marketplace. Similarly, they must communicate workers' compensation program benefits to employees recognizing that benefit levels and conditions will vary from state to state. The complexity of these communications must be taken into account, and the message should be simplified to the extent possible.

Third, employees today often face information overload. Different departments sometimes issue competing objectives. Travel frequently takes people away from the workplace. Employees receive conflicting messages on television, the internet, and a host of other media. Examples are the television commercials encouraging injured workers to seek legal counsel or the chiropractor advertisements found on outdoor boards, bus benches, or telephone directory covers. Risk managers must compete within this noisy environment and find creative means for promoting their message.

Marketing and Sales Strategies

Given these types of challenges and the potential claims dollars at stake, many progressive companies view strong risk management communications as an essential part of their self-insured programs. They understand the value of promoting and selling the cost management programs they have put in place. It is this type of marketing and sales mentality that drives successful communications campaigns within an organization and ultimately leads to lower workers' compensation costs.

They understand the value of promoting and selling the cost management programs they have put in place. It is this type of marketing and sales mentality that drives successful communications campaigns within an organization and ultimately leads to lower workers' compensation costs.

In creating effective risk management communications campaigns, risk managers should utilize the same promotional techniques that their marketing and sales counterparts use in promoting and selling the company's products and services. Some of the key communication elements risk managers will want to focus on are: target marketing, core message, and distribution channels.

Target Marketing. One of the first areas risk managers will want to address is target marketing. Risk managers must understand their audience and their respective corporate agendas and then create messages specifically for these population segments.

For example, manufacturing people are interested in production issues; human resources people are interested in personnel issues; financial people are interested in bottom line issues. If risk managers are to successfully sell their cost management programs, they must show these various groups how these programs benefit them and help advance their corporate cause. Clearly, manufacturing groups are interested in higher production and less downtime; human resources groups are interested in a fully engaged and healthy workforce; and financial groups are interested in lower insurance and claims costs.

Key Communication Concepts
- Target Marketing
- Core Message
- Distribution Channels

In creating effective risk management communications campaigns, risk managers should utilize the same promotional techniques that their marketing and sales counterparts use in promoting and selling the company's products and services.

Another way risk managers can segment their audience is based on seniority, experience, and position. For example, senior executives, middle managers, and employees approach workers' compensation issues with different interests. Top tier executives are interested in such issues as lower costs, productive workforce, and corporate image. Middle managers are typically interested in the impact of workers' compensation practices on production and sales goals. Associates and employees are interested in performing their job duties within the confines of a safe workplace and the availability and level of benefits should an accident occur.

Core Message. The development of a core message is an activity which should be given a great deal of thought. The core message is comprised of the central themes which are to be conveyed. While individual messages should be tailored to reflect the interests of each audience segment identified, the core message will exhibit some common elements. In the case of workers' compensation, employees at all levels and within all departments should have a sense of what workers' compensation is, how the system operates, its impact on the organization, and the benefits to which injured employees are entitled.

People need to understand that workers' compensation has a long history and was initially introduced in the United States during the early 1900's. Its purpose was to guarantee some level of wage replacement and medical care to injured workers and their families. At that time, few workers had the financial means to seek legal recourse in response to a workplace accident. Such an accident often depleted resources and placed an extreme hardship upon workers and their families.

Originally, the workers' compensation system was based upon the no fault and exclusive remedy principles. In other words, an injured worker was entitled to receive workers' compensation benefits without having to prove an employer's negligence. In turn, benefits were limited to those prescribed by law. It was believed this type of system would guarantee some means of financial security for workers and eliminate potentially expensive and uncertain outcomes

In the case of workers' compensation, employees at all levels and within all departments should have a sense of what workers' compensation is, how the system operates, its impact on the organization, and the benefits to which injured employees are entitled.

posed by legal actions in a court of law. Such a system was designed to benefit both the employee and business owner.

Employees should also understand the financial impact of workers' compensation upon their organizations. Workers' compensation costs and corresponding insurance prices are on the rise. These, in turn, affect a corporation's profitability and financial outlook. Resulting costs may weigh even more heavily during challenging economic times. These communications become even more powerful when savings can be related to impact on earnings per share. Similarly, some companies relate a specified amount of losses to the additional production or sales needed to mitigate these loss amounts. As companies seek to fine tune their financial strategies, more attention is paid to cost management measures and means for maintaining a productive workforce. A successful self-insurance program can help achieve these goals by lowering costs, preventing accidents, and reducing downtime.

> *Marketing and communications skills are as essential to the risk management discipline as underwriting and financial analysis. These are the skills needed to launch a successful risk management communications campaign and will ultimately drive the success of the cost management programs which are put in place.*

It needs to be reiterated to employees today that workers' compensation benefits are determined by law, and benefit levels and conditions vary by state. Some frequently asked questions include: When do benefit payments begin? How much money will I receive? Will I be in trouble for reporting a claim? Which doctor can I see? Will I have a job upon recovery? Should I seek the advice of an attorney? Answers to these and similar questions are often best communicated prior to an employee suffering an accident at the workplace.

Distribution Channels

Once a core message is defined, risk managers must determine how best to convey this message to their target audiences. Fortunately, there are more means of message distribution today than ever before. These include employee orientations, ongoing education and training meetings, internet and CD-ROM programs, digital videos, and print material campaigns including educational brochures, posters, and corresponding communications. Direct communication from an employee's immediate supervisor is probably the single most effective technique. Successful programs use a mix of these elements in reaching their audiences.

Message Distribution Channels
- Employee orientations'
- Ongoing education and training meetings
- Supervisor communications
- Internet and CD-ROM programs
- Digital videos
- Educational brochures, posters, and correspondence
- Print communications

Like all successful advertising and marketing campaigns, creativity is essential. Professional development and design should be utilized to enhance the effectiveness and delivery of the message. Creating a strong brand will help reinforce message identity and establish equity in these communications. Strong emphasis should be placed on message frequency and message consistency.

Why does an employee need to know all of this information? First, it hurts to get hurt. Second, it costs the company money when employees get hurt, and prices go up. Third, if prices go up too much, jobs disappear.

Marketing and communications skills are as essential to the risk management discipline as underwriting and financial analysis. These are the skills needed to launch a successful risk management communications campaign that will ultimately drive the success of cost management programs.

Recognizing the high stakes associated with a self-insurance program, many progressive companies are beginning to give risk management communications the attention it deserves.

CHAPTER FOURTEEN:

Conclusion

CHAPTER OVERVIEW: *Through the years, self-insurance has assumed a position of prominence within the risk management and insurance industry. Today's difficult market conditions once again have elevated interest and turned the spotlight toward self-insurance plans. A well-designed and well-managed self-insurance program can achieve many valuable benefits for an organization. Self-insurance can address a wide range of risk management challenges and should be considered regardless of the state of the economy or insurance market.*

TODAY'S MARKET CONDITIONS HAVE ONCE AGAIN THRUST SELF-INSURANCE INTO THE SPOTLIGHT. Most organizations are presently facing rising insurance prices and shrinking insurance capacity. As a result, financial executives, risk managers, brokers, and other industry professionals need to have an understanding of self-insurance and related concepts.

The key lies in businesses being able to understand and look for ways to maximize program benefits and minimize program disadvantages based upon their current conditions and circumstances.

Most self-insured companies share a common goal in wanting to gain greater control over their risk management programs. Additionally, the potential for immediate cost savings, insulation from market cycles, and increased safety and claims awareness often outweigh any perceived disadvantages associated with this type of program. The key lies in businesses being able to understand and look for ways to maximize program benefits and minimize program disadvantages based upon their current conditions and circumstances.

Once a self-insurance program is established, active management and performance measurement are crucial to long-term success. Particular emphasis should be placed on analyzing risk management data and information, establishing a strong safety culture, streamlining the claims management process, and launching a successful communications campaign. These types of actions truly enable a self-insured entity to control its own destiny.

Once a self-insurance program is established, active management and performance measurement are crucial to long-term success.

Remember Keisha Greene, the aggressive CFO who was considering self-insurance as a means of strengthening the company's financial position? She has successfully implemented a self-insurance program and is now capitalizing on investment income opportunities offered by such a plan.

Remember Scott Malone, the resourceful broker who introduced the concept of self-insurance to his client who was facing significant premium increases? He has solidified his relationship with his client as a result of the creativity and value he offered this company.

Remember Michael Sanchez, the risk manager who was exploring self-insurance as a means of gaining greater control over his company's claims activities? Self-insurance has allowed him to create a claims culture more sensitive to employee needs while exercising greater control over costs.

Self-Insurance: Is it the right solution for your risk management challenge? You owe it to yourself to find out. ∎

State and Territorial Rules and Regulations: Contact Information

For current information on state and territorial regulations regarding self-insurance and workers' compensation, it is important to go to the source. The contact information provided below is believed to be correct as of the date of publication, but see also the *Workers' Compensation Administrators Directory* compiled by Robert W. McDowell for the North Carolina Industrial Commission:

http://www.comp.state.nc.us/ncic/pages/all50.htm#pr

The U.S. Department of Labor's overview, *State Workers' Compensation Laws,* is available at:

http://www.dol.gov/esa/regs/statutes/owcp/stwclaw/stwclaw.htm

Alabama

Workers' Compensation Division.
Industrial Relations Division
649 Monroe Street
Montgomery, AL 36131
334-242-2868
http://www.dir.state.al.us/wc

Alaska

Division of Workers' Compensation
Dept. of Labor & Workforce
P. O. Box 25512
Juneau, AK 99802-5512
907-465-2790
www.labor.state.ak.us/wc/wc

Arizona

Industrial Commission of Arizona
800 West Washington Street
Phoenix, AZ 85007-2922
602-542-4411
www.ica.state.az.us

Arkansas

Workers' Compensation Commission
324 Spring Street
Little Rock, AR 72203
501-682-3930
www.awcc.state.ar.us

California

Department of Industrial Relations
Office of SI Plans
2265 Watt Avenue, Ste 1
Sacramento, CA 95825
916-483-3392
www.dir.ca.gov/sip

Colorado

Division of Workers' Compensation
1515 Aprapahoe Street, Tower 2, Suite 500
Denver, CO 80202
303-575-8700
www.coworkforce.com/dwc

Connecticut

Workers' Compensation Commission
Capitol Place
21 Oak Street
Hartford, CT 06106
860-493-1500
wcc.state.ct.us

Delaware

Department of Labor
Office of Workers' Compensation
4425 N. Market St., 3rd Floor
Wilmington, DE 19802
302-761-8200
www.delawareworks/divisions/industaffairs/diaindex

District of Columbia

Department of Employment Services
Office of Workers' Compensation
77 P Street NE, 2nd Floor
Washington, DC 20002
202-671-1000
www.does.ci.washington.dc.us/services

Florida

Division of Workers' Compensation
Dept. of Labor & Employment
211 Hartman Bldg.
2012 Capitol Circle SE
Tallahassee, FL 32399
850-488-2514
www.doi.state.fl.us/wc

Georgia

State Board of Workers' Compensation
270 Peachtree Street, NW
Atlanta, GA 30303-1299
404-656-3875
www.ganet.org/sbwc

Guam

Workers' Compensation Commission
Department of Labor
504 D. Street
Tiyan, Guam 96910
671-475-0101
www.gov.gu

Hawaii

Disability Compensation Division
Dept. of Labor & Industrial Relations
P. O. Box 3769
Honolulu, HI 96812
808-586-9151
www.dlir.state.hi.us

Idaho

Industrial Commission
317 Main Street
Boise, ID 83720
208-334-6000
www2.state.id.us/iic

Illinois

Industrial Commission
100 West Randolph Street, 8-200
Chicago, IL 60601
312-814-6611
www.state.il.us/agency/iic

Indiana

Workers' Compensation Board
402 West Washington Street, Room 196
Indianapolis, IN 46204
317-232-3808
www.state.in.us/wkcomp

Iowa

Iowa Division of Workers' Compensation
1000 E. Grand Avenue
Des Moines, IA 50319
515-281-5387
Internet: www.state.ia.us/iwd/wc

Kansas

Division of Workers' Compensation
800 SW Jackson Street, Ste. 600
Topeka, KS 66612-1227
785-296-3441
www.hr.state.ks.us/wc

Kentucky

Department of Workers' Claims
1270 Louisville Road, Bldg. C
Frankfort, KY 40601
502-564-5550
www.kylabor.net/workcomp.htm

Louisiana

Department of Labor
Office of Workers' Compensation
1001 N. 23rd Street
Baton Rouge, LA 70802
225-342-7555
www.ldol.state.la/us

Maine

Workers' Compensation Board
27 State House Station
Augusta, ME 04333
202-287-3751
www.state.me.us/wcb

Maryland

Workers' Compensation Commission
10 East Baltimore Street
Baltimore, MD 21202-1641
410-864-5100
www.charm.net/~wwc

Massachusetts

Department of Industrial Accidents
600 Washington Street, 7th Floor
Boston, MA 02111
617-727-4900
www.state.ma.us/dia

Michigan

Bureau of Workers' and
Unemployment Compensation
P. O. Box 30016
Lansing, MI 48909
517-322-1296
www.michigan.gov/bwuc

Minnesota

Workers' Compensation Division.
Department of Labor & Industry
443 Lafayette Road
St. Paul, MN 55155
651-284-5005
www.doli.state.mn.us/workcomp

Mississippi

Workers' Compensation Commission
1428 Lakeland Drive
Jackson, MS 39296-5300
601-987-4200
www.mwcc.state.ms.us

Missouri

Division of Workers' Compensation
3315 West Truman Boulevard
Jefferson City, MO 65102
573-751-4231
www.dolir.state.mo.us/wc

Montana

Workers' Compensation Regulation Bureau
1805 Prospect Avenue
Helena, MT 59624-8011
406-444-5600
erd.dli.state.mt.us/workcompreg

Nebraska

Department of Insurance
941 "O" Street, Ste. 400
Lincoln, NE 68508-3639
402-471-2201
www.nol.org/home/ndoi

Nevada

Division of Industrial Relations
400 West King Street, Suite 400
Carson City, NV 89703
775-684-7260
dirweb.state.nv.us

New Hampshire

Workers' Compensation Division
State Office Park
95 Pleasant Ct.
Concord, NH 03301
603-271-3176
www.labor.state.nh.us

New Jersey

Division of Workers' Compensation
P. O. Box 381
Trenton, NJ 08625-0381
609-292-2515
www.state.nj.us/labor

New Mexico

Workers' Compensation Administration
2410 Centre Avenue, SE
Albuquerque, NM 87125-7198
505-841-6000
www.state.nm.us/wca

New York

Workers' Compensation Board
20 Park Street
Albany, NY 12207
518-474-6670
www.wcb.state.ny.us

North Carolina

Industrial Commission
Dobbs Building, 6th Floor
430 N. Salisbury Street
Raleigh, NC 27603-5937
919-807-2500
www.comp.state.nc.us

North Dakota

North Dakota Workers' Compensation
500 East Front Avenue
Bismarck, ND 58504-5685
701-328-3800
www.ndworkercomp.com

Ohio

Bureau of Workers' Compensation
30 West Spring Street
Columbus, OH 43215-2256
614-644-2950
www.ohiobwc.com

Oklahoma

Workers' Compensation Enforcement Division
4001 N. Lincoln
Oklahoma City, OK 73105-4918
405-528-1500
www.okdol.state.ok.us/workcomp

Oregon

Department of Consumer & Business Services
Workers' Compensation Division
350 Winter Street NE, Room 27
Salem, OR 97301-3879
503-947-7810
www.cbs.state.or.us/wcd

Pennsylvania

Bureau of Workers' Compensation
1171 South Cameron Street, Room 324
Harrisburg, PA 17104-2501
717-772-4447
www.dli.state.pa.us

Puerto Rico

Industrial Commissioner's Office
P.O. Box 364466
San Juan, PR 00936
787-783-3808
www.cipr.gobierno.pr

Rhode Island

Workers' Compensation Division
1511 Pontiac Avenue, Building 69, 2nd Floor
Cranston, RI 02920-4407
401-462-8100
www.dlt.state.ri.us/webdev/wc

South Carolina

Workers' Compensation Comm.
1612 Marion Street
Columbia, SC 29202
803-737-5700
www.wwc.state.sc.us

South Dakota

Division of Labor & Management
Department of Labor
Kneip Building, Third Floor
700 Governors Drive
Pierre, SD 57501-2291
605-773-3681
www.state.sd.us.dol

Tennessee

Department of Commerce & Insurance
500 James Robertson Parkway
Nashville, TN 37243
615-741-2241
www.state.tn.us/commerce

Texas

Workers' Compensation Commission
Southfield Bldg.
4000 South IH 35
Austin, TX 78704
512-804-4100
www.twcc.state.tx.us

Utah

Labor Commission
P. O. Box 146600
Salt Lake City, UT 84114-6600
801-530-6800
www.labor.state.ut.us/indacc

Vermont

Department of Labor & Industry
National Life Building, Drawer 20
Montpelier, VT 05620-3401
802-828-2286
www.state.vt.us/labind

Virgin Islands

Department of Labor
Workers' Compensation Division
302 King Street
Frederiksted, St. Croix, VI 00840
340-692-9390

Virginia

Workers' Compensation Commission
1000 DMV Drive
Richmond, VA 23220
804-367-8600
www.vwc.state.va.us

Washington

Department of Labor & Industries
273 Linderson Way, SW
Olympia, WA 98504-4001
360-902-4200
www.wa.gov/lni/insurance

West Virginia

Bureau of Employment Programs
Workers' Compensation Division
4700 Mac Corkle Avenue, SE
Charleston, WV 25304
304-926-5000
www.state.wv.us/bep

Wisconsin

Workers' Compensation Division
Department of Workforce Dev.
201 E. Washington Ave., RM C100
Madison, WI 53707-7901
608-266-1340
www.dwd.state.wi.us/wc

Wyoming

Workers' Safety & Compensation
Department of Employment
122 West 25th Street, 2nd Floor
East Wing, Herschler Bldg.
Cheyenne, WY 82002-0700
307-777-7159
wydoe.state.wy.us

Self-Insurance Associations and Statistical Resources

Self-Insurance Associations

- National Council of Self-Insurers (NCSI)
  PMB 345
  1253 Springfield Avenue
  New Providence, NJ 07974
  908-665-2152, fax 908-665-4020
  E-mail natcouncil@aol.com
  www.natcouncil.com

- Self-Insurance Institute of America, Inc. (SIIA)
  12241 Newport Avenue
  Suite 100
  Santa Ana, CA 92705
  714-508-4920, fax 714-508-4904
  E-mail webmaster@siia.org
  www.siia.org

Organizations Providing Informational and Statistical Resources

- Integrated Benefits Institute (IBI)
  525 Market Street
  Suite 740
  San Francisco, CA 94105
  415-222-7280, fax 415-222-7281
  E-mail info@ibiweb.org
  www.ibiweb.org

- National Academy of Social Insurance (NASI)
  1776 Massachusetts Avenue, NW
  Suite 615
  Washington, DC 20036
  202-452-8097, fax 202-452-8111
  E-mail nasi@nasi.org
  www.nasi.org

- NCCI - National Council on Compensation Insurance, Inc.
  901 Peninsula Corporate Circle
  Boca Raton, FL 33487
  561-893-1000, fax 561-917-7025
  E-mail customer_service@ncci.com
  www.ncci.com

- National Safety Council (NSC)
  1121 Spring Lake Drive
  Itasca, IL 60143-3201
  630-285-1121, fax 630-285-1315
  E-mail customerservice@nsc.org
  www.nsc.org

- U.S. Bureau of Labor Statistics
  Postal Square Building
  2 Massachusetts Avenue, NE
  Washington, DC 20212-0001
  (202) 691-5200, fax (202) 691-6325
  E-mail feedback@bls.gov
  www.bls.gov

- UWC – Strategic Services on Unemployment & Workers' Compensation
  1201 New York Avenue, NW
  Suite 750
  Washington, DC 20005
  (202) 682-1515, fax (202) 842-2556
  E-mail info@uwcstrategy.org
  www.uwcstrategy.org

- Workers Compensation Research Institute (WCRI)
  955 Massachusetts Avenue
  Cambridge, MA 02139
  (617) 661-9274, fax (617) 661-9284
  E-mail wcri@wcrinet.org
  www.wcrinet.org

Other Books on Self-Insurance and Related Topics

The library of professional literature on risk management is rich, but book-length treatments of self-insurance are few. Leading insurance and risk management periodicals are important sources for specialized discussions, and new ideas often surface first at industry conferences. General texts on insurance and risk management are also helpful as introductions that place self-insurance within the context of other loss funding techniques. Below is a selection, by no means comprehensive, of recent survey texts on risk and insurance as well as a few specialty treatments of self-insurance and related workers' compensation issues.

Boyce-Smith, John and Pearce, Alan M. *Practical Self-Insurance: An Executive Guide to Self-Insurance for Business.* San Francisco; Risk Management Press, 1985.

Brandon, Lawrence G. *Let the Trumpet Resound: The Insurance Industry in the 21st Century.* Malvern, Pennsylvania: CPCU-Harry J. Loman Foundation, 1996.

Conder, Joseph M. and Hopkins, Gilbert M. *The Self-Insurance Decision.* Montvale, New Jersey: Institute of Management Accountants, 1981.

Dorfman, Mark S. *Introduction to Risk Management and Insurance.* Upper Saddle River, New Jersey: Prentice Hall Professional Technical Reference, 2001.

Douglas, Janet R., ed. *Integrated Disability Management: An Employer's Guide.* Brookfield, Wisconsin: International Foundation of Employee Benefit Plans, 2000.

Elliott, Michael W. *Risk Financing.* Malvern, Pennsylvania: Insurance Institute of America, 2000.

Greenwood, Judith and Taricco, Alfred, eds. *Workers' Compensation Health Care Cost Containment.* Horsham, Pennsylvania: LRP Publications, 1992.

Harrington, Scott E. and Niehaus, Gregory R. *Risk Management and Insurance.* New York: McGraw-Hill Higher Education, 1998.

Head, George L.; Elliott, Michael W. and Blinn, James D. *Essentials of Risk Financing.* 2 vols. 3rd ed. Malvern, Pennsylvania: Insurance Institute of America, 1996.

Head, George L. and Horn, Stephen, II. *Essentials of Risk Management.* 2 vols. 3rd ed. Malvern, Pennsylvania: Insurance Institute of America, 1997.

Quinley, Kevin M. *Claims Management: How to Select, Manage, and Save Money on Adjusting Services.* Horsham, Pennsylvania: LRP Publications, 1992.

Rejda, George E. *Principles of Risk Management and Insurance.* Boston: Addison-Wesley, 2002.

Trieschmann, James S.; Gustavson, Sandra G. and Hoyt, Robert E. *Risk Management and Insurance.* Mason, Ohio: South-Western College Publishing, 2000.

U.S. Chamber of Commerce Statistics and Research Center. *2002 Analysis of Workers' Compensation Laws.* Washington, D.C.: U.S. Chamber of Commerce, 2002.

Vaughan, Emmett J. and Vaughan, Therese M. *Essentials of Risk Management and Insurance.* Hoboken, New York: John Wiley & Sons, 2002.

Welch, Edward M., ed., *Workers' Compensation: Strategies for Lowering Costs and Reducing Workers' Suffering.* Fort Washington, Pennsylvania: LRP Publications, 1989.

Related Source Materials and Articles also by Catherine D. Bennett, CPCU, ARM

"Good Loss Control Culture Cuts Costs," *National Underwriter,* August 16, 1998.

"Controlling Job Related Stress Claims," *Global Risk Manager,* April 1995.

"Drug Industry Trends Help Employers", *National Underwriter,* February 6, 1995.

"How to Curb Workers' Comp Costs," *National Underwriter,* June 25, 1990.

"Large Deductible Plans vs. Self-Insurance," *National Underwriter,* July 22, 1991.

"Workers Compensation Costs: Qualified Self-Insurance Provides Maximum Control," *Business Insurance,* March 11, 1991.

"Self-Insureds Can Curb WC Losses," *National Underwriter,* August 27, 1990.

"How Risk Managers Should Choose TPAs," *National Underwriter,* June 25, 1990.

"Risk Managers Consider Self-Insuring WC Cover," *National Underwriter,* April 30, 1990.

"Containing Work Comp Costs – Apply Tools Used On Medical Plans," *Business Insurance,* February 26, 1990.